A Hard Day's Night

Samira Ahmed

THE BRITISH FILM INSTITUTE
Bloomsbury Publishing Plc, 50 Bedford Square, London, WC1B 3DP, UK
Bloomsbury Publishing Inc, 1359 Broadway, New York, NY 10018, USA
Bloomsbury Publishing Ireland, 29 Earlsfort Terrace, Dublin 2, D02 AY28, Ireland

BLOOMSBURY is a trademark of Bloomsbury Publishing Plc

First published in Great Britain 2026 by Bloomsbury on behalf of the
British Film Institute, 21 Stephen Street, London, W1T 1LN
www.bfi.org.uk

The BFI is a cultural charity, a National Lottery distributor, and the UK's lead organisation for film
and the moving image. We believe society needs stories. Film, television and the moving image
bring them to life, helping us to connect and understand each other better. We share the stories
of yesterday, search for the stories of today, and shape the stories of tomorrow.

A catalogue record for this book is available from the British Library.

A catalog record for this book is available from the Library of Congress.

ISBN: PB: 978-1-8390-2939-4
         ePDF: 978-1-8390-2941-7
         ePUB: 978-1-8390-2940-0

Printed and bound in India

For product safety related questions contact productsafety@bloomsbury.com.

To find out more about our authors and books visit www.bloomsbury.com
and sign up for our newsletters.

BFI Film Classics

The BFI Film Classics series introduces, interprets and celebrates landmarks of world cinema. Each volume offers an argument for the film's 'classic' status, together with discussion of its production and reception history, its place within a genre or national cinema, an account of its technical and aesthetic importance, and in many cases, the author's personal response to the film.

For a full list of titles in the series, please visit
https://www.bloomsbury.com/uk/series/bfi-film-classics/

Contents

Acknowledgments

I am indebted to Mark Lewisohn for his scholarship and advice, and to Chris Shaw for inviting me onto his podcast *I Am the Eggpod*. Also to David Janson, John Bloomfield and Jonathan Clyde for their generosity. Thank you to the BFI's librarians and film archivists, the Goethe-Institut in London for their help on the German version of the film, to my family, especially my brother Salim for introducing me to the Beatles, Elodie Harper, Will Page for the music and Philip Lawford for boarding the train for the adventure.

Introduction

If an alien were to land on Earth, a watch of *A Hard Day's Night* (hereafter *AHDN*) would provide a pretty good snapshot of what was going on culturally in Britain in 1964. There were half-demolished buildings, class divides, pompous men in charge, an entertainment culture dominated by a strange combination of highbrow opera and lowbrow variety, and lots and lots of screaming children and teenagers fixated on four young male musicians in suits with thick dark mops of hair. The screaming might confuse them.

Many adults would have felt a bit like aliens in their own land at the takeover of Beatlemania, a term that first appeared in print in

Press photocall at Twickenham Film Studios, 12 March 1964 (Schoolgirls from left: Pattie Boyd, Tina Williams, Prue Berry, Susan Whitman) (photograph by John Rodgers)

October 1963. It was a period when so much was changing so fast. The Profumo affair had embarrassed the upper classes and challenged the class deference that still endured. Peter Cook's The Establishment club and the TV satire show *That Was the Week That Was* (1962–3) had been feeding some of that energy into entertainment culture on stage and screen. But the Beatles were at its epicentre. On 4 November 1963 at the Royal Variety Performance in front of the Queen Mother and Princess Margaret, John Lennon invited the people in the posh seats to 'rattle yer jewellery'. From March 1964, pirate radio would start to challenge paternalistic controls over the dissemination of youth culture by broadcasting pop music presented by young DJs directly into British homes.

A major influx of young Commonwealth immigrants, my parents among them, were bringing their skills, their cuisine and their culture to cities like London. The capital was a unique cultural melting pot, with transatlantic talent shaking up the offering at ITV and BBC Television.

The new head of BBC Drama, Sydney Newman, commissioned *Doctor Who* (1963–). George 'Bud' Ornstein of United Artists and former publicist Walter Shenson were among the Hollywood studio affiliates making successful British films, including the comedy *The Mouse That Roared* (1959), with British stars such as Peter Sellers. There was New York ad man Robert Brownjohn, who projected images onto curvaceous female bodies for the memorable opening title sequences of *From Russia With Love* (1963) and *Goldfinger* (1964), for their producers, Harry Saltzman and Albert 'Cubby' Broccoli. And another ad man, with no knowledge of pop, but a love of surreal comedy and jazz – Richard Lester – was finding plenty of work as an ad director, selling Smith's Crisps with the help of a cheerful young blonde model called Pattie Boyd, to cross-subsidise his bouts of filming cinema and TV comedies, even an Oscar-nominated short, *The Running, Jumping & Standing Still Film* (1960), shot over two weekends for £70.

Richard Lester on location during the making of *AHDN* (photograph by Bert Cann)

A coming together of some of these North American men (Ornstein, Shenson and Lester) would put a new, more youthful version of British manhood on the big screen for the first time. Their film would have the crisp black-and-white cinematography and documentary style of the new social realism, but also the slapstick of golden age silent comedy; and with the Beatles' black polo necks and handsome faces, the freewheeling sexiness and youthful energy of the French *nouvelle vague*. Filmed partly with the new lightweight cameras, it would be a race against time, made on a modest budget, shot partly on the hoof, with mistakes and accidents deliberately left in, pieced together with songs written in snatches while the Beatles were doing their day job of concert performing. Even the title emerged late in the shoot from a verbal joke that then required a title song to go with it, written overnight in the final days of filming. The result was the film *A Hard Day's Night*.

To anyone born in the late 1960s or early 70s, the Beatles existed as a kind of deep folklore in black and white. Their early TV appearances seemed from another world. I have an early memory of seeing Beatles archive on TV and being puzzled that I didn't know who they were. When I finally found out, a piece of the jigsaw of Britishness finally slotted into place, but I also felt a sense of having missed out on something huge.

Like thousands of British children of that generation (we hadn't yet been designated Generation X) born to Commonwealth parents from South Asia, the West Indies or East Africa, who were sometimes treated like aliens, I found film and television culture a vital part of understanding the small island nation of my birth and its remarkable cultural power. In the 1970s my mother, Lalita Ahmed, would journey up to Birmingham's BBC television studios every week to host programmes in Hindustani, such as *Naya Zindagi: Naya Jeevan* (New Life) (1968–82) and the women's programme *Gharbar* (1977–87), for South Asian immigrants trying to find their place in this new land. She would also show Brits how to cook real Indian food at home through her cookbooks and live cookery slot on the daily magazine show *Pebble Mill at One* (1972–96), where she would also get to meet the entertainment stars *du jour*, such as Sacha Distel. This was recognisably the same world that had fostered Richard Lester in the 1950s, with laughing camera crews and accidents happening in the rush of live TV. Once she took me to watch proceedings from the director's gallery. I loved it and would later make my own career in live broadcasting, though in news rather than entertainment.

The daytime shows my mother worked on weren't, of course, aimed at me. Instead, with an elder brother born in 1963, I grew up heavily influenced by the 1960s pop groups Salim loved and the mixtapes he made for me. My father, Athar – always a keen early adopter – bought our first home video recorder in 1975. And at Christmas 1979 when the BBC scheduled a Beatles film season on the 'arty' channel BBC2, my brother recorded them all on our Betamax recorder and, aged eleven, like so many others before and since, I fell under their spell.

I would come home from school and put on a Beatles film at least a couple of times a week before starting my homework. *AHDN* and *Help!* (1965), especially, were a kind of time tunnel to an eternal Saturday afternoon feeling of adventure. A Britishness that was about cocking a snook; like the black-and-white Ealing comedies and the old Hollywood slapstick films that padded out TV schedules. I didn't yet know the director of *AHDN* and *Help!* was himself a huge fan of Buster Keaton and an immigrant. But thanks to his films I met John, Paul, George and Ringo – 'the gang to end all gangs, self-sufficient, witty and all-inclusive',[1] who made me feel welcome.

Forty years later, as a woman in my early fifties, I found myself suing the BBC for equal pay over years of sex discrimination. Getting on the train home after my first day of giving evidence, I thought instinctively of the opening of *AHDN* and listened to the album every day travelling to and from the employment tribunal hearing; on the train, walking across Waterloo Bridge. With passers-by of all ages and backgrounds stopping to wish me luck, I felt an emotional bond with the film and the Britain that the Beatles represented in it. Cocking a snook. I won my case.

Over the years since I first watched *AHDN*, I have caught up on much of the acclaimed cinema of the 1960s, and it was a shock to realise how many British New Wave films of the era had dated, sometimes terribly, often because of their portrayal of women or race. Even the Beatles' follow-up, *Help!*, featured some light-hearted brownface. The original *AHDN* script had a scene of questionable racial humour, which was excised before shooting began. How had *AHDN* avoided such pitfalls, especially when viewed from the far more politically self-aware 2020s? And why has its reputation grown to attain a kind of elite status in cinema? The film critic Alexander Walker identified it as one of only four genuinely original British films made in the 1960s, alongside *Blow-Up* (1966), *If....* (1968) and *Performance* (1970).[2] This seemed a good line of inquiry.

New insights have come from talking to actor David Janson, who played the young truant in the film, and to three of the young women hired as extras for the opera and concert sequences, about the reality of a hard day's singing and screaming for the cameras.

With the huge growth in Beatles scholarship in recent years, I was wary of adding another book. Three things gave me the confidence. First was appearing on Chris Shaw's warm-hearted Beatles podcast *I Am the Eggpod*, where I discussed my theories about the film and found an audience interested in my ideas about the wider cultural and social history behind it.

Second, in 2023, was the impact of my story of the Beatles concert at the exclusive English boys' boarding school, Stowe – thanks to student John Bloomfield's generosity in sharing his tape recording from April 1963 with me. The history of that moment was so rich and joyful in its juxtaposition of music, class, popular culture and social change. That edition of BBC Radio 4's *Front Row* (1998–) enthralled listeners, who weren't necessarily Beatles fans.[3]

Ad-libbing for a cinema trailer at Twickenham Film Studios, 3 April 1964 (photograph by Bert Cann)

Finally, there was the release of the Disney+ *Beatles '64* documentary in 2024, which revisited the Maysles brothers' footage of the band's first US visit. Shot for Granada TV just three weeks before they began filming *AHDN*, the parallels and contrasts between fact and fiction in their material offer valuable insights for an up-to-date reassessment of *AHDN*.

This is not a dry book of film theory, though I have plenty of theories about the film. I hope it will appeal both to Beatles fans, who have so much knowledge of the band, and to those readers whose interest lies in the power of the moving image. After all, the band are never directly named in the entire picture.

A big vogue in my 1970s childhood was the practice of burying time capsules full of toys and gewgaws of the day, to be dug up and puzzled over in the future. As this book will explore, *AHDN* was made in a rush, to bottle something – a new teen craze – that most people, including the film's producers, assumed would soon dissipate. Yet strangely, as each year passes, even though it is absolutely of the moment, the film has not dated. We will see how *AHDN* was in fact a kind of cinematic Big Bang, shaping entire genres of screen entertainment: sitcoms, rock band films and spawning a new format – the pop video, for which in 1984 MTV gave Richard Lester a special Vanguard Award. He jokingly demanded a paternity test.

AHDN is that impossible thing: an exhumed mystery of a lost era, like Tutankhamun's tomb, but still alive, fizzing with energy.

1 Watching *A Hard Day's Night*

It's going to be a far-out story. And it will be in black and white because the Beatles are black and white people.

Film producer Walter Shenson, 1963[4]

Before we settle down to watch the film through, I want to think about where (if you were too young to catch the original cinema release) you might have first seen *AHDN* and the place it occupies in our hearts as comfort viewing.

It was of course released on video cassette in the 1980s. I saw it crop up at revival house screenings in the US and Germany throughout the 1990s. It was remastered and re-released on DVD and on cinema screens for its fiftieth anniversary. And it still pops up reliably on the BBC iPlayer streaming service, with its 87-minute runtime infinitely pausable, and re-runnable. Strangely, it often feels like it has an equally loved twin on the BBC TV Saturday afternoon schedules: the Cliff Richard musical *Summer Holiday* (1963), which came out in January that year, just at the point when the Beatles were close to becoming the biggest cultural phenomenon in Britain.

The Beatles had watched Cliff's career carefully – he was about the same age, but four or five years ahead in fame and success, and they learned from it. His debut hit, 'Move It' (1958), and his recordings with the Shadows, undoubtedly influenced the Beatles' own thinking about songwriting and musicianship. Cliff's inability to break America was one of the reasons they didn't want to go to the US until they'd had a hit single there. What could we learn from watching *Summer Holiday*?

Well, *Summer Holiday* also opens in black and white, in the pouring rain no less, with an icon of Britain's transport system – the red London Transport double-decker bus. The move from black and white to colour is one of the great joys of the film. Cliff plays one of a gang of four working-class friends – all mechanics employed by London Transport. The comedy plotline of a scheming showbiz mother trying to mess up their plans is merely a more elaborate version of Paul's Irish grandfather nonsense. Their plan to drive to the South of France captures all the aspirations of 1960s Britain: glamorous foreign travel to the home of the *nouvelle vague*, picking up female 'talent' along the way. But the film was made to a Hollywood formula and it showed.

Melvyn Hayes, who played Cyril, says his hair was dyed blond because executives said there was always a blond buddy like the actor Van Johnson.[5] *Summer Holiday* was made to help Cliff Richard break through in the US. Even though it was a hit at the time, it lacks the biggest ingredient the Beatles had in spades: authenticity. It took an American who loved Britain to realise that nothing could or would be more exciting to Americans, or anyone, than the Beatles as they were. And in *AHDN* Richard Lester made Britain feel like the most exciting place to be in the world. Cliff Richard's follow-up to *Summer Holiday*, *Wonderful Life* (1964), featured more idyllic beaches and escapism (this time in the Canary Islands), but was weak by comparison to its predecessor, and critics said as much. It premiered on 2 July 1964, four days before the *AHDN* premiere, a coincidence that, like a planetary alignment, could be seen as a sign of his eclipse by the Fab Four.

So, now we are ready to press play on *AHDN*. It's often described as a fictionalised thirty-six hours in the life of the Beatles, as they travel down by train from Liverpool to London for a live TV show, but really, it is several films in one: a current affairs documentary about a new pop phenomenon, but shot like a wildlife documentary – these four playful, long-legged creatures with their irresistibly watchable antics. It's a surreal TV sitcom with no laughter track. It's a war film of a commando unit heading from mission to mission, diving in and out of trains and helicopters as they go – all captured by a cinematographer who shot aerial combat footage as an RAF cameraman in World War II. Two-thirds of the way through it becomes, for a while, a social realist drama, with two troubled working-class boys meeting on a towpath. And it is also what it is not – a classic 'let's put on the show right here!' pop musical, as pioneered in 1930s Hollywood, with a grumpy old curmudgeon threatening to ruin everything. This was a familiar plot premise in recent British films such as *The Young Ones* (1961) and Richard Lester's own *It's Trad, Dad!* (1962) (see Chapter 2).

But, above all, it is a French *nouvelle vague*-style frolic in the spirit of Truffaut or Godard. This is no country for old men, is the first thought that hits you as the film opens on a crashing discordant chord and shortly after, the first of a spate of casualties.

There is a quick introduction for new users as we appear to be in the middle of a chase down an alleyway: the confident one (John) running first; another, slimmer and darker (George), hand in pocket, is grinning as he looks over his shoulder at the laughing crowd of youngsters racing after them; and a third (Ringo), shorter, close behind – all with dark jackets and thick mops of hair.

Suddenly, George trips – as he falls, his right hand emerges from his pocket just in time stop his face hitting the pavement. Ringo crashes heavily on top of him, but they're soon up and racing onwards. Even through the adrenalin rush, George can't help but look down and rub his wrist a little. That must have hurt.

We cut to a wide shot of a grand Edwardian station glass canopy and the main entrance to Marylebone railway station, where these young men are heading, all L. S. Lowry stick men legs, followed close behind by that cartoon cloud of children. And this time it's one of the young girls taking a tumble – she rolls hard on the ground, by the archway.

Into the concourse now and our first hint of the surreal: the three are suddenly in phone booths watching the blur rush by. Communications in the form of phone and photo booths, newspapers, ad hoardings and magazines – all surround every shot of the Beatles as they rush through the station, with (later on) press and television cameras zooming in, following their moves in much of the film.

A HARD DAY'S NIGHT

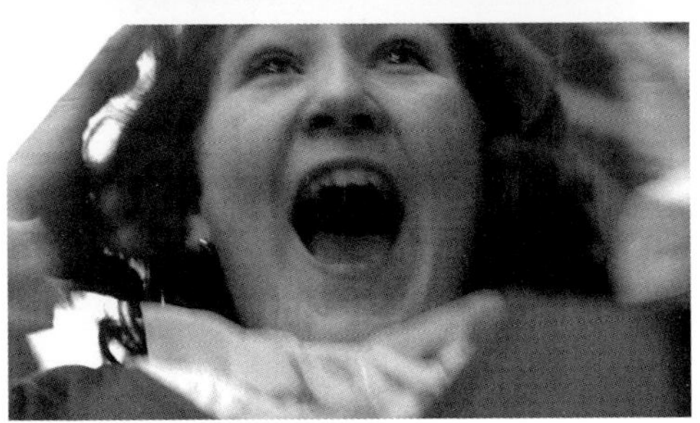

We are caught up in the hunt in closer confines; the boys are the prey. John looks out of a café window warily and we cut away to the face of a screaming girl – she's spotted them. A tally ho! in this new urban world of girls as hunters and young men as foxes.

In a dead-end alley lined with newspaper hoardings they are trapped and left to improvise a way out, watched by a bemused waiter. There is a sense of the boys' self-awareness in this version of their daily reality semi-staged for the camera; placed in scenarios with the camera watching how they'll find their way out. They hoist themselves up and over the hoardings, offering a glimpse of their lithe bums in those tight trousers. Landing on a moving newspaper cart, as if in a James Bond film escape sequence, John leaps off it and they are next seen bounding over metal barriers – the first of many running, jumping and (fewer) standing-still moments.

Lester directing the Beatles' escape over the hoardings (photograph by Bert Cann)

John, George and Ringo are suddenly relegated to background characters running past, while our attention is drawn to a bench. Behind a large newspaper the camera zooms in to find Paul, with a trad jazz beard, sitting next to Wilfrid Brambell's Grandfather, looking at a copy of the pin-up magazine *Men Only*.[6] He is that 'dirty old man' in the catchphrase used by his on-screen sitcom son in *Steptoe and Son* (1962–74). The show was the biggest thing on British TV at the time, drawing audiences of more than twenty million.[7]

The boys take refuge in a photo booth, and we see the madness from their point of view, with the crowds of pursuing fans reflected in the mirror outside the booth. John and Ringo watching them go by and deciding to make a run for it. We, like the camera, are trapped on the wrong side of the booth and cannot follow. Instead, the camera captures the geometric field of the station canopy and concrete floor, with these three angular figures moving through it like points on a radar screen.

We cut to a close-up of a huddle of girls – their round faces like bubbles of eagerness.

By one minute fifty-nine seconds we are building to a climax. At the far end of the platform with Grandfather and Paul, we watch the approaching tsunami – a dark, boiling, duffel-coated, cardiganed cloud of waving arms and legs and heads, emitting screams and cheers that we cannot yet hear above the engine of that pounding song. A group of girls are elbowing each other for room – on the edge of a fall themselves – trying to avoid tripping over a camera operator's dolly being pulled just ahead of their feet. Another casualty – a boy in a duffel coat is down and rolling at speed under the relentless juggernaut of legs.

Two minutes thirty seconds in and the departing whistle blows and we hear the real sound of the crowd screaming – a high-pitched wave of noise that we will repeatedly encounter from now on. In the sea of faces that has suddenly gathered, we can make out elderly ladies, newspaper men with giant camera flashbulbs, uniformed railway staff, including a white woman and a Black man. It is a snapshot of modern, fast-changing Britain, glimpsed through the eyes of the Beatles.

But hang on, where did the little old ladies and snappers appear from? The shot was captured by director Richard Lester, instinctively driven to seize the opportunity, without regard for continuity. And with it the viewer has experienced their first orgasmic Beatles encounter through a catchy new song, turned into a visual adventure. The comforting chug chug of the wheels of the train in motion has us in post-coital calm, ready to get better acquainted with the four young men who inspired such frenzy. We haven't even been told their names.

There is no sense of the Beatles checking each other out or laughing about their escape or catching their breath. No concession is made for what we've just been through as the viewer. We are already fully with the Beatles inside their bubble – the reserved sticker on the window of the first-class compartment the only sign that they might have special status.

Sitting down inside, George is reading the paper, but otherwise the band confront each other in the moment, like actors in a play performed in the round. The windows, the mirrors on each wall,

Ringo fiddling with a camera continue the idea that they are constantly seen through a set of glass viewfinders, establishing a quasi-proscenium arch of performance.

The idea of the band as a kind of single entity with a hive mind begins with the Mexican wave-style wordless communication as, nudged and nodded, they assess the little old man in their midst and we can assess them – their individual suits and especially their fabulous hair, nothing like the ludicrous identical black floppy pudding-bowl mops with which they are usually impersonated.

Olivia Arias, future wife of George Harrison, was a sixteen-year-old California teenager when the film came out. She says the importance of their hair on screen can't be overestimated. American men had never looked like that. It was a thrilling rebellious challenge to the strict conformity of the aggressively masculine preppy or sports jock cropped hair of boys at school.[8]

Paul and Grandfather eye each other coolly, as if aware of each other's celebrity status. One from TV, the other from the new world of youth culture. Paul offers a half-wink of acknowledgment. Brambell sits stiff and erect like an intruder in their world, which he is. It's an image that will repeat often through the film.

Some critics, including Stuart Maconie, have made the case that the film would be better without Brambell's presence. The constant references to his being a 'clean old man' – an obvious play on the Steptoe catchphrase – suggest a sleazy male perspective. This is even clearer in the novelisation of the film, which is told more overtly from his point of view. Screenwriter Alun Owen justified Brambell's presence as a catalyst: 'a codgy old man … to try and divide the brotherhood'.[9] The casting was more about a wider (older) audience appeal. As a character, though, he fills the same laboured role as Robert Morley, playing the mean old dad to British heart-throb Cliff Richard in *The Young Ones*.

Watching the film as a child, unfamiliar, like most international viewers, with the sitcom, the reference passed me by but felt tonally part of the mood created by Owen's arch dialogue. There is a British social realism comedy feel throughout, with a loving repetition of 'swine' rather than 'pig', and argumentative riffing. And there is in *AHDN* a sense of Owen giving them a stylised version of themselves. Grandfather, we are told, is 'nursing a broken heart'. 'He'll cost you a fortune in breach of promise cases,' says Paul. Throughout the film non-Scousers may not quite get the exact words, but we get the tone, and they cast an incantatory effect.

Combing his hair while he explains Grandfather's presence (Mother 'thought a change would do him good'), Paul is clearly established as the matriarch in a classic sitcom formula, explained by comedy writer Joel Morris as Matriarch, Patriarch (John), Craftsman (George) and Clown (Ringo). As Morris points out, the band often spoke of how they only truly became the Beatles once Ringo joined; once they had their clown.[10]

Each new member of the team is introduced to the compartment, setting up the dynamics of the Beatles' wider sitcom family. John Junkin as Shake – their dogsbody assistant – was modelled on their real-life assistant Mal Evans. Junkin was a veteran of Joan Littlewood's Theatre Workshop and went on to be a foil for Tony Hancock. His genial comic presence helps ameliorate any appearance of nerves among the Beatles on screen. They trust Shake.

'Got on all right?' he asks, as he hands out snacks and drinks. 'No,' says John solemnly. Shake is relaxed – like an experienced mum, he knows how to handle them. Together with road manager Norm (Norman Rossington), they are an older generational layer of sitcom matriarch and patriarch.

Norm warns against trouble, while the four each start playing, displaying their own tics: George diving into the crusty roll in the paper bag, Paul nodding responsibly as if listening, John playing with the bag straps and sniffing the Pepsi bottle. The 'veiled cocaine reference!' gets a mention in the 1984 BBFC (British Board of Film Classification) viewing notes for VHS release, but 'should probably go safely over the heads of the very young', thereby protecting the film's U certificate.

The presence of Grandfather is questioned again and again, drawing a collective response about him being very 'clean'. In a real sitcom this point would have added or been expected to generate (canned) audience laughter. Instead, we get silence and the continuing rattle of the train on its tracks. The impact is a feeling of weirdness to proceedings. This is not a sitcom, or a documentary. Quite what, we don't know.

The arrival of a bowler-hatted, suited older gent with a briefcase and newspaper changes the atmosphere. It's an encounter so many of us have had as teenagers or children. The handheld camera follows him in documentary style, as he blocks the exit and commands Norm and Grandfather to 'make up your mind'. His hat falls off the rack initially – the first of many such moments of 'vérité' that enhanced the feel of something real unfolding. The boys, helpful and smiling, wish him a good morning. He gives a look of haughty horror, complete with eye roll, and then hides in his broadsheet newspaper, finding himself surrounded by a manifestation of a social menace he's read about in its pages.

But equally, there's a sense of them all eyeing each other up, like cartoon characters getting ready for a fight. John looks cool but calculating. Underrate him at your peril. He is, we can tell, the most unpredictable and dangerous of the four.

The gent takes a second to clock the small open window and rises to close it, as if to establish ownership of the compartment. Ringo gasps 'woah!', looking at George, both recognising a perfect moment of passive aggression on public transport. It is so English and so class-infused. They aren't going to pretend they didn't notice.

Paul very politely points at it and asks, 'do you mind if we have it open?' 'Yes, I do,' comes the strong reply. City Gent is ready for this, his sense of entitlement in no doubt. The group goes into action – all for one. John's tone hints at menace – 'There's four of us' – but then he suddenly bats his eyelashes, girlishly, to wind him up. The gent's response – 'I travel on this train regularly twice a week' – feels real because it is. 'The thing on the train really happened to us when

the man came in and closed the window and put the radio off,' Ringo
Starr later recounted. 'And we told Alun ... and he put it in.'[11]

As in the real encounter, Ringo turns on a portable radio,
only to have the gent turn it off and double down on his moral
superiority, citing his knowledge of the Railways Act. Paul cosies up,
listening, as if to humour him; Ringo looks stunned, while George
scowls darkly. And then Paul reveals the left-leaning politics of the
Beatles: 'We're a community. Majority vote. Up the workers and all
that stuff.'

John, silent till now, moves his face in close like Rod Hull's
unpredictable creature Emu. Will he attack? But he says only, 'give us
a kiss.' The psychology of the scene rings true. After John points out
the older man's childishness, saying to Paul that 'you can't win with
his sort. After all it's his train,' City Gent, warming to his sense of
victory, turns to John and hectors him: 'And don't take that tone with
me, young man. I fought the war for your sort.'

Ringo leans forward to deliver the sassiest line in the film:
'I bet you're sorry you won.' It has the extra joy of gifting the Beatles
a kind of resolution they never had in real life. But it's a takedown of
an attitude that was constantly being deployed at the time, especially

The confined reality of filming at the compartment door (photograph by Bert Cann)

as the Beatles represented the first age group to narrowly miss compulsory National Service.[12]

Like Billy and his friend's high-kicking dance routine on the war memorial in *Billy Liar* (1963), the scene is more startling viewed from the perspective of modern Britain, in which an unquestioning veneration in any reference to World War II seems ingrained in the news media. At a time when more vicious class satire was on our screens in Joseph Losey's *The Servant* (1963) or Clive Donner's *Nothing But the Best* (1964), the Beatles are winning the class war with charm, rather than viciousness.

The Beatles underscore their moral victory by leaving, in Paul's words, 'the kennel to Lassie'. They pull childlike faces at the compartment door, asking for their ball back, as if schoolboys with a mean old neighbour.[13] And then we are presented with the film's first fully surreal episode, when the four somehow suddenly appear outside the window, running alongside the train, on foot or bicycle, banging at the window and repeating their plea. It's followed by Ringo being carried sideways through the corridor like a parody of a wipe sequence into the next scene. From here on, we know for

Shake watches as the Beatles look at their old image

sure whose side we're on, and we know we can't be sure what will happen next.

In a film in which the Beatles are frequently reproduced through camera viewfinders, studio monitors, TV set backdrops of beetles and leaping life-size blow-ups, one image keeps recurring: the pile of old photos Grandfather carries around. While it acts as a simple plot thread about his being on the make, it represents something more important. That image of the Fab Four in those famous collarless jackets spawned a thousand pop band imitators and was used on the cover of the first *Beatles Book* monthly fan magazine in August 1963. But it's already obsolete and represents the static past. They've long moved on. Keep up, Grandad!

In the buffet car, we see the boys as ordinary young men were usually portrayed at the time – heterosexual, warm-blooded and keen to 'pull' the talent they see sitting down for coffee. While the two women cast were actually nineteen at the time, only two years younger than George, the image of these knee-socked sixth-formers in school uniform tunics is, by modern standards, discomforting. In fact, Lester gives a relatively innocent presentation, compared to the overtly sexualised way teenage schoolgirls were portrayed in mainstream culture at the time. There had been three popular films based on the Ronald Searle *St Trinian's* cartoons by 1960. Model Pattie Boyd would have been somewhat familiar to teenage audiences, as the Smith's Crisps girl in print ads and a TV commercial. Filming the scene also provided one of the most famous and meta meet-cutes in cinema history, with George asking Pattie – his future first wife – out.[14]

George offers Paul an elaborate horse-racing metaphor as cautionary advice. The boys are starting to warm up into the strange dialogue. Paul even borrows a bowler hat from somewhere and heads off to flirt with the girls. Grandfather intervenes to claim the boys are convicts and the ladies should 'get out while you can!' Boyd's sole line in the film, a quizzical 'prisoners?', is, of course, a truth of the Beatles' existence.

'I'd ask you out meself, only I'm shy' (photograph by Bert Cann)

As Shake reads his *Mad* magazine book, time slips by, with the
Beatles spread across the train, hunting *From Russia With Love*-
style for Grandfather. It's worth watching how the Beatles move
through the corridors. Paul lithely, Ringo smoking and doing a kind
of Groucho Marx chicken walk, complete with a dead stop to view a
glamorous lady through the glass partition. George walks more stiffly,
geekily even, but winks madly at the woman, after Ringo refuses to
be drawn by her beckoning finger.

By contrast John and Paul swing into a compartment full of
schoolgirls – classmates of the two we've already met. There's a sweet
sense of *Candid Camera*-style improv as the girls start pulling their
hair and gasping, too startled to scream. John gurns like a toothless
old lag, possibly even a 'dirty old man' ('I bet you can't guess what I
was in for …'), Paul dragging him out, apologising.

Longer scenes about Grandfather's 'engagement' were dropped and we soon cut to the guard's carriage, where Paul is keeping watch over him, confined. The other Beatles turn up, giving the sense that they are unable to stay apart for long. John suggests a game of cards to pass the time, uttering a Tarzan-style grunt as the schoolgirls arrive to watch them.

And here we witness the invention of the pop video, the vision of editor John Jympson, as the intro to 'I Should Have Known Better' fades in, timed to Ringo's comedy card dealing. It was the first time the sound preceding the song sequence had been overlaid in this way. George starts tapping his feet and nodding, Paul begins to mime along with the lyrics while in the card game, as if they're all listening to the song on the radio. John's hand is at one moment throwing down cards, then raising a mouth organ to his lips. We are in a parallel timeline in which the band are playing their instruments round the same crate.

Other pop video templates will be created in this film, but this one establishes perhaps the most familiar template of the 'dual scenario' – cutting between the band performing the song and the alternative action plot (in this case, the card game). A prominent example is the Go-Gos' video for 'Our Lips Are Sealed' (1981), in which a performance on a stage is intercut with them driving around in a car and larking about in a fountain.

The edit lingers on close-ups of their eyes and fringes, matching the Robert Freeman imagery of the album, film poster and end titles. And the elegance of these familiar handsome faces is playfully contrasted with the brooms and fire buckets, rattling inches away.

Camerawork with a wide pan round the rear of the cage delights in presenting the band in a kind of mini circus ring of performance for each other, seen through the wire mesh or spokes of the wheel – a visual trope Lester and cinematographer Gilbert Taylor often used in *It's Trad, Dad!* While they are technically the trapped animals, it's the girls who seem confined on the wrong side of the cage. As we see again and again through the film, they are only truly

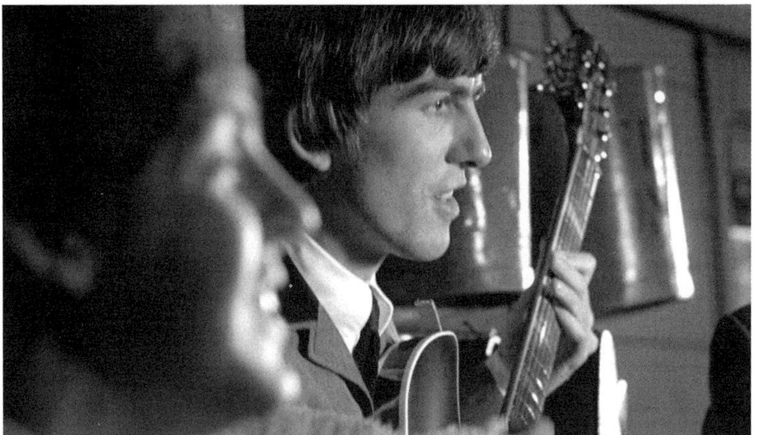

free in their music. This sequence was filmed at Twickenham Studios, with studio hands rocking the carriage, to simulate the train's motion. Lester had to stop and restart shooting as they began rocking in time to the song.[15]

Grandfather at one point even seems to be straining to mime alongside Paul, like a grandad watching him on TV. As the camera cuts to hands fighting over the game of cards, we're back out of the music dream and into the film story. There's a clear pleasure in the camera catching their expressions: Paul deadpan as if shocked, Ringo grinning as he examines his hand, Paul winking as he's gifted a card in this madness of made-up moves.

The song fades and after two and half minutes of musical escape, train sounds re-emerge, as we hear the rhythm of the train slowing to a halt. The screaming crowd is waiting outside. We recognise that sound now. Identical to what they left behind. Once you know that the band will arrive at the same Marylebone station they 'departed', it adds a little cinematic irony. It's all the same wherever they go.

There is a moment of pause as the Beatles and their manager plot an escape like a military operation through the line of taxis to their waiting car. These moments of endless dodge and escape that punctuate the film were captured by Taylor, who had filmed Allied bombing raids for wartime prime minister Winston Churchill, and had come from the military satire of *Dr. Strangelove* (1964) to film *AHDN*. Editor Jympson, who had worked on many British war films, had recently edited *Zulu* (1964), which displays a very different sense of British boys under siege.

We watch the flow of girls around the taxis, like a swarm of bees in a nature documentary. Lester does nothing to the footage, other than let it run. This is the fluid mechanics of Beatlemania in action.

As the Beatles' car swings out of the station, we cut to the view from inside, reminiscent of the New York car mayhem at the airport, captured in the Maysles brothers' footage in *Beatles '64*. The boys are laughing at the chaos outside. We spot one girl rapping on the rear windscreen before being dragged off. The last shot of this sequence picks out an older woman in skirt suit, handbag, gloves and court shoes, running with the children, but giving up as the car speeds off, as if aware of the camera behind her. Not a paid extra, but a little glimpse of the multi-generational fascination the band aroused.

Plink plink. The sound of Paul noodling on the piano opens up an image of a quiet oasis in their hotel and John reading a magazine claiming to contain the 'first scientific survey of the greatest pop groups'. Shot on a sound stage at Twickenham Studios, it is the biggest fiction of all. *Beatles '64* revealed the band always under siege, their rooms overcrowded with camera crews, equipment and hangers-on. By contrast, this is a very gentle fantasy version of their existence, and one that might appeal to school-age fans: Norm bringing in their fan mail and, like a firm parent, telling them he wants it answered tonight.

Ringo's first envelope is an invitation to a private casino, a scenario that had occurred in Manhattan, with a very keen George pushing but failing to convince their management to allow them to accept a VIP invite to Manhattan's Playboy Club. In the film version of himself, Paul, who in real life was dating the upper-middle-class actress Jane Asher and living with her family, has a rather effective joke in which he appears not to know how to pronounce 'buffet'.

'Chemin de fer, baccarat and champagne buffet' (photograph by Bert Cann)

Led by John, the troublemaker, the four immediately disobey orders and head off for a night out. An authentic, if highly sanitised version of the truth. It's a chance to watch the boys at play, with the feel of a fly-on-the-wall documentary. There was no shortage of this kind of footage, as middle-class current affairs broadcasters tried to make sense of youth culture. But here, we are mercifully free of any patronising RP (received pronunciation) voiceover. The music plays loudly over the top so we can only guess at their conversation. This is definitely an older crowd than the schoolgirls on the train.

It's Ringo, acknowledged to be a great dancer, who throws himself into things with selfless clowning abandon as he and George improvise a boxing move – is this a new craze they've just invented? Are they mocking the idea of dance crazes? The scene has uncanny similarities with a nightclub visit in *Beatles '64*, in which Ringo is in the swing of things with two very smart young women – while middle-aged DJ Murray the K tries too hard alongside him. *AHDN* lacks the excruciating embarrassment of watching a figure quite so deluded as to his hipness. The tall and gangly Jeremy Lloyd – the future co-creator of sitcoms *Are You Being Served?* (1972–85) and *'Allo 'Allo!* (1982–92) – is Ringo's duelling partner on the dance floor. The sprinkling of comedy writers and performers throughout this film and *Help!* (in which Lloyd also appears as a customer in the Indian restaurant), intercut with Grandfather's shenanigans in the casino, 'earthed' the Beatles' glowing sexual charge in the world of English TV comedy. Their animal edge is still there, but you could choose to miss it, distracted by the gags.

Both the nightclub and casino scenes were shot on location on two days, a month apart, on different floors of the same club building: Les Ambassadeurs and the Garrison in Hamilton Place, Mayfair.

Lester and Owen added more scenes for individual Beatles as their on-screen confidence grew, particularly for George, whose laconic presence is a real discovery of the film. The bathroom shaving scene was just such an addition, shot at Twickenham Studios

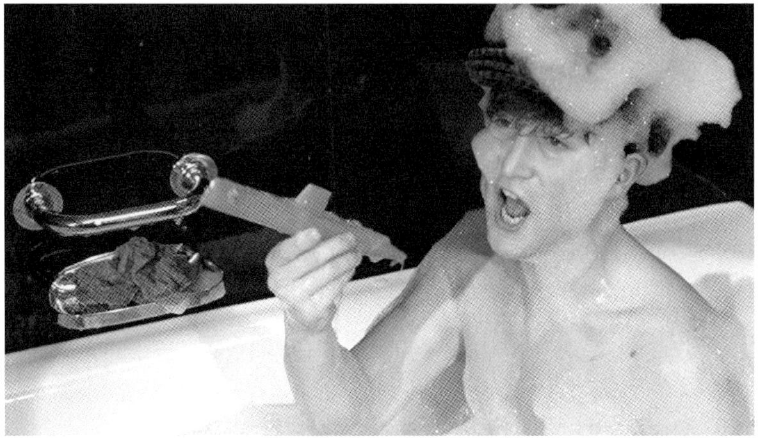

on 13 April, the same day as George's later solo adventure in the ad agency. The morning after the night's adventures, we find John playing Goon-like submarine games and speaking cod German in the bath, while George agrees to show Shake how to wet shave using his reflection in a mirror. The German dub of the original film replaced the World War II references with John having a pretend phone conversation with the shower head attachment. Both George and Junkin play their scene dead straight, while John larks in the bath. Lester adds another surreal moment when Norm, pulling out the plug, fears he's lost John down the plughole.

The now familiar military operation required when the Beatles head anywhere is presented in brief, as their car pulls up outside the Scala Theatre in Fitzrovia, the location of their TV special later that day. An elaborate traffic jam sequence with fantasy cowboy Western dialogue was deleted.

Once inside the theatre foyer, the four scatter again, like an upturned jar of insects, transforming every space they enter with their restless energy. A single camera follows them on the move into the hall, up the staircase and out, all in the same frame: Paul and Ringo start to sit down, John is talking non-stop, teasing a press official about the man's handkerchief, George curls up and pretends to go to sleep, Paul points around and refers to someone taking them as hostages.

The press conference scene was shot and improvised days earlier than scheduled, after a crowd of excited fans and a consequent police order issued to the crew to leave made their planned exterior shoot impossible. Filmed at the Scala Theatre on Thursday 2 April, two days after they shot *AHDN*'s climactic concert sequence, it was partly inspired by their press conference at JFK airport, fielding inane questions about their hair, and the bizarre reception they had endured at the British Embassy in Washington DC in February. They had been deeply shocked at how rudely they were treated by embassy staff and the posh attendees, and by an incident there, in which a fan had produced scissors and cut off a lock of Ringo's hair.

Lester used the theatre bar, calling in 'two or three people that I knew, but a lot of them were actual journalists or journalists' wives doing the interviews … Because we didn't have time to cast it.'[16]

From the opening frames of the scene that foreground the bottles of drinks and snacks, we are seeing as if through the eyes of the Beatles. For thirty-five seconds we hear no audible dialogue, just the wildlife-style hubbub of clinking glasses and journalists' chatter. Gradually, the Beatles' voices fade up out of the burble – a pop art montage out of the footage, deliberately mismatching question and answer.

A dark-haired, older woman, clearly flirting with Ringo, light-heartedly raises the only topical subject that dates the film to 1964 – 'Are you a mod or a rocker?' It was only three days since the Easter weekend clashes between groups of mods and rockers and police in Clacton-on-Sea had stirred up a national moral panic in the newspapers about delinquent youth.

George, mugging for the camera and pulling cartoon faces, inspires on screen a lovely frame-by-frame contact sheet animation, complete with the sound of shutter clicks. A glimpse of John's uncensored raciness comes when, asked about his hobbies, he

carefully writes (follow the pen strokes) – but we do not quite see – the word 'tits' on the female reporter's notebook, raising a gasp. Another woman grins as she reads it over her shoulder.

As Paul's attempt to grab a beer is blocked by yet another question-babbling journalist with a microphone, we see John, Paul and George as the hungry hostages they are, shooting eyebrow semaphore to plot their escape. It is a lovely Lester touch that

'Just passing through, like'

the press pack don't even notice the Beatles disappear, as if down
a plughole.

As the four walk into the theatre stalls, Lester takes a moment to
delight at the world of TV prepping below. Camera crews, set movers
and costumed dancers all bustle about on stage. Watching the Beatles
rush through the director's gallery, we get our first brief glimpse of
actor Victor Spinetti as the director, oblivious to their passing behind
him. He's a key character, who has yet to make his official entrance
in the film. It's a lovely *nouvelle vague* touch as Lester and the Beatles
defy the traditional rules of film-making, jumping ahead of the plot
and how characters are normally introduced.

We cut to a shot of the Beatles' drum kit; the one moment in
the film – apart from the concert finale lights – when we see the band
name. It is never spoken. While a studio workman sweeps the stage
in one of those long coats that defined the 1960s factory floor, John
launches into a rendition of 'If I Fell', delivered as if to cheer Ringo
up. A more complicated set-up in the original script was ditched and
instead we just get the business of TV rehearsal happening around
them. When George leans on the amp Shake has just plugged in,

Victor Spinetti with the floor manager (Robin Ray): 'I see it all now, it's a plot. A plot' (photograph by Bert Cann)

it slips on its stand with an audible thump, but they continue with a grin. Again, there is the sense of fly-on-the-wall documentary style, as they discuss improvements after the playthrough.

When Spinetti walks on – a nervous figure in a polo neck and fluffy mohair sweater – he looks every inch the highly strung arty director he was cast to play; an extreme version of Lester himself. Spinetti recalls that the scene developed out of Lester's habit of taping when he said they were rehearsing. He was recording the very first walk-on rehearsal where Spinetti introduces himself to the band, and John declares, 'You're not a director', only an actor pretending to be a director. Spinetti said, 'I kept going and I said I am a director. I have an award on the wall in my office.' 'A likely story,' retorts John, and raises his eyebrows.[17]

In his few lines Spinetti establishes himself as a rather fragile representative of the Establishment, already finding his nemesis in John's hard stare, and seeking the aid of 'a bottle of milk and some tranquillisers' for what promises to be a bumpy ride.

After a slapstick gag with comic actor Derek Nimmo, an encounter with an actor in eighteenth-century Georgian costume offers a fine moment of camp exchange as he and John check each other out. There's a hint of Julian and Sandy-style banter – the camp couple who would soon feature in the popular BBC radio comedy show *Round the Horne* (1965–8).

John heads up a spiral staircase pretending to grope like a dirty old man at chorus girls heading downwards. Norm tells him to 'put them girls down or I'll tell your mother of you'[18] – the others silently grin as they check out the talent themselves. Lester conveys the sense of the band as straight young men, by the then acceptable comedy standards of the day (though John is, arguably, also mocking the leering male norm of light entertainment culture), and without any overt romance plot. Although knowledge of the men's romantic partners was in the public domain, the Beatles' manager Brian Epstein went along with the convention of artist managers at the time, with female fans in mind, to preserve the fiction in the film of

the boys as single. Visually, Lester builds a powerful contrast between the low ceilings, narrow corridors and spiral staircases, and the break-out to open sky above the fire escape. As Norm keeps talking like a parent-cum-jailer about locking them in until they're required again, the boys spot an exit door and seize their moment. 'We're out!'

Running down the fire escape to 'Can't Buy Me Love', the Beatles are as French *nouvelle vague* as they will ever be. The camera swirls around with them in circles on the angular stairs forming Bridget Riley-like pop art geometrical patterns through the metal lattice squares with their Cuban-heeled boots – the Beatles refracted to their essentials. A recognisable Lester trademark was using pop art-style pixelation, and this sequence has echoes of the Temperance Seven scene he shot through a screen in *It's Trad, Dad!* At the bottom of the stairs they leap over broken bits of Victorian-looking scenery – the remains of a chariot and lamps, a stringless harp – a symbolic running away from the detritus of old Britannia.

The sequence is the most complex of the film and partly the result of serendipity, shot in three different locations weeks apart (aerials at Gatwick airport on 13 March, the fire escape at the Hammersmith Odeon on 22 April and larking around at ground level

Lester directing the larking about on a mocked-up helipad at Thornbury playing fields (photograph by Bert Cann)

on a mocked-up helipad at Thornbury playing fields in Isleworth on 23 April). The helicopter – booked to shoot the final shots of the film when they depart after the concert – had to be hired for the whole day, so once that shot was in the can, the watching crowd at Gatwick was told that shooting had ended to get them to disperse. After lunch the Beatles changed outfits, and Lester came up with a list of three things for them to do and set them off.[19] Gilbert Taylor was experienced at filming from a moving aircraft but realised once up in the air that the camera battery was running low and therefore the camera was undercranked. This meant the film ran through the camera at a slower frame rate than expected, creating, when it was played back at normal speed, an unplanned but pleasing speeded-up 'silent film' style.[20]

They used stepladders, held in place by one of the electricians, to leap into the air – captured like flying squirrels in wildlife

(Photograph by Bert Cann)

documentary slo-mo by the camera operator lying virtually horizontal on the ground. The images echo the memorable jumping pop photography of Fiona Adams, which featured on the cover of their 1963 *Twist and Shout* EP.

Richard Lester had directed two TV comedy series for ITV – *A Show Called Fred* and *Son of Fred* (both 1956), written by the anarchic comedian and actor Spike Milligan. Lester was hugely influenced by his surreal style, and this sequence is full of Milligan-esque plays on British schoolboy rituals. There is a mock sports day race and the playground-style boxing match with Ringo counted out and pretend-kicked as he lies on the ground. Paul gets to be himself, grabbing the camera as he appears to scream, timed to sync with his Little Richard vocalisation in the song.

In a play on Busby Berkeley dance films, Paul, Ringo and George appear as three kaleidoscopic dreaming heads in a circle, eyes closed as if talking in their sleep or reciting prayers or making wishes: a hive mind and offering another angle on those amazing heads of hair – all sharp curls and fringes.

John had to leave the Isleworth shoot early for a Foyles literary luncheon, but the edit masks that. It's Lester's feet and POV

holding the camera in the do-si-do sequence between the 'four'. John is therefore absent from the final shot of the sequence when a groundsman in cloth cap and wellington boots tells them to get off what is 'private property'. A hint of class war! Authority-defying George appropriately delivering the sarcastic riposte: 'I'm sorry we hurt your field, mister.'[21]

As the Beatles re-enter the gloomy theatre corridors, John is spotted by Millie, played by Anna Quayle in her first film role (see Chapter 4 on women). In a beautiful piece of writing about celebrity, the figure John resembles, like the Beatles themselves, is never named out loud. Lester doesn't allow the scene to be stagey or slow; in its short duration there walk through a Napoleonic uniformed soldier ('Noddy'), various chorus girls and a man carrying a double bass.

If *AHDN* begins and ends in earnest documentary style, it's worth noting that its very centre (the scene in the ad agency is exactly halfway through the running time) is a deliberate dive into the essence of fakery. George, in search of a canteen, wanders into an advertising agency casting a new campaign for shirts aimed at the teen market. A young man is sitting in reception as George walks past

'Don't breathe on me, Adrian.' Simon's assistant (Julian Holloway) has recognised George

– the 'fake' version of George's real thing. The environment speaks of pretentious office decor – the abstract painting and the ugly metal sculpture that George twangs with his guitarist's instinct.

For a film full of irony, it is an extra serving to know that camp, superficial southerner Simon was played by Kenneth Haigh, who had been the original 'angry young man' – a phrase coined by the Royal Court Theatre's own PR – the first actor to play Jimmy Porter in John Osborne's play *Look Back in Anger* (1956). Appearing in *Caligula* at London's Royal Court at the time of shooting *AHDN*, Haigh chose not to be named in the film's credits, fearful it might damage his prospects as a serious actor.

Lester makes a hard cut from this cynical scene to a TV rehearsal of Johann Strauss II's popular 1874 operetta, *Die Fledermaus*, in full nineteenth-century costume, presumably part of

(Photograph by Bert Cann)

the same TV show line-up as the Beatles. Spinetti is bobbing his head along in the same way he does to the Beatles. It is all a set-up for one of Lester's memories of TV accidents – Grandfather, accidentally appearing through the trapdoor. Many of the singers for this shoot were students from the Royal Academy of Music, recruited by word of mouth and paid £10 for the day. They only had to learn about eight bars and filmed several different takes. During the lunch break some of the singers, still in their dirndl-skirted peasant costumes, plucked up the courage to go over and ask the Beatles for autographs. 'Do you come from haunts of coot and hern?' Paul said to one, quoting Alfred Tennyson's 'The Brook', a poem then widely taught in British schools.[22]

A cameo next for the Beatles' tailor Dougie Millings, who waits with an anxious nail-biting Norm in the band's dressing room. Plotwise, it sets up Ringo's disillusionment, but the brief scene is engaging for how the band appear to start fiddling at once with everything and everyone. John pretends to be a lady dignitary snipping the ribbon on a bridge opening. He did many different takes, offering a different response each time.

'Where are they?' A highly strung Spinetti paces the floor, awaiting the Beatles. When they arrive they mock him mercilessly, as he retreats to the booth, but a few seconds later, on his brief cue – 'er, music' – their personal tensions disappear and we are transported into cinematic sincerity as the ballad 'And I Love Her' strikes up. So much of the charm of this film is in such transitions between the comedy on the (TV) factory floor and the on-camera polish of the performances.

The edit lingers on them refracted through the wall of gallery and camera monitors. The effect is a pop art celebration, with Paul captured from every angle, like a sequence of Andy Warhol screenprints. In contrast to the faster songs elsewhere, this ballad is matched with slow mixes, a loving close-up of Ringo's hands on the bongos and George tenderly embracing his Spanish guitar. It's Paul's moment in the spotlight, as the troubadour of love, with a flare light enveloping him in an eclipse-like cosmic event, complete with halo.

Gilbert Taylor explained later that the high-contrast black
and white was to hide the dirty set. The revolving shot of Paul was
deliberately experimental: 'We were also shooting directly into 10K
lamps behind them, using the intense light to explode the image and
make things as exciting as they could be.'[23] It is the 'white heat of
technology', to quote Harold Wilson's famous Labour conference
speech, captured in this film just a few days after the Labour leader
met the Beatles at a Variety Club lunch.

The sequence ends with the camera pulling out to reveal the
full artifice of the studio set: arc lights, boom mics, monitors, cables
and all. Having drawn us into experiencing our own semi-religious
encounter with the band, we are pulled back from our reverie to
acknowledge the technological role of the medium in the message.
The director's polite tannoy announcement 'thank you, very nice'
captures both the professional protocol of TV and Lester's instinct to
undercut any sentimentality.

In the make-up room, shot in a confined space with extras
all around, and composed in the edit, the scene captures elements
of the Beatles' real-life personalities in little flashes: Paul's actor-y
spoof of *Hamlet*, complete with comic-book exclamation and his

direct-to-camera 'zap!' George spouts more scripted witticisms at a make-up girl, while John threatens to punch an arrogant singer, who backs off rapidly. Ringo, by contrast, is more of the outsider, playing the part written in the screenplay as George accuses him of sulking. Grandfather delivers the line about seeing nothing more than 'a train and a room and a car and a room and a room and a room' that was the seed for Alun Owen's whole script. He was inspired by seeing the Beatles on the road in Dublin and how confined they were wherever they went. Grandfather also delivers his 'considered opinion that you're all a bunch of sissies' – a version of which would probably have been heard by many of the audience from the patriarchs in their own families and workplaces.

Back on the stage, Lionel Blair and his dancers are on their toes to a jazz version of 'I'm Happy Just to Dance with You' in front of backdrops of beetle illustrations, mocking the literalness that characterised much light entertainment culture. Blair remembers that Lester wanted the scene to evoke the sense of them performing at the London Palladium. The original script suggested a wild dance-off but, recalls Blair, the band didn't want to dance.[24] Instead, we see only John jumping around wildly. The Beatles head over to pick up

their instruments and join in. John cheerfully mocks the traditional pop music film, declaring, 'Let's do the show right here!' as they launch into 'I'm Happy Just to Dance with You'.

With its loving pull-out from the viewfinder of camera 2, this sequence is the apotheosis for me of what I call the 'eternal Saturday afternoon' energy of the film. Make-up girls watch, as Blair and his dancers are still choreographing their moves behind them. Lester treats this song in a wholly different way to every other so far: not an official performance or rehearsal, they are playing for each other, facing inwards. The Beatles are often shown grinning and looking around, aware of what's happening. Paul even raises an eyebrow, exchanging a glance with Ringo, as they watch the make-up girls being dragged off by their supervisor. A focus pull makes Ringo's drumsticks flutter like insect wings in front of John's face.

The canteen scene starts with us picking out Grandfather and Ringo with a zoom-in on Grandfather's bored face. It's a moment for Lester to linger on the fun of the TV factory, with costumed performers carrying their food trays, a Nazi with his gun on the table, one tending to his stage wound with a little extra ketchup.

(Photograph by Bert Cann)

Ringo is reading the novel *Anatomy of a Murder* (filmed by Otto Preminger in 1959) as Grandfather embarks on a lecture about the joys of 'parading' over reading. Owen's script has a Joe Orton-esque sense of masculine fantasy, as he coaxes Ringo into heading off on his own. 'You could be out there betraying a rich American widow, or sipping palm wine in Tahiti, before you're too old like me.' So rich is the speech that it's possible to entirely miss the visual gag constructed around its delivery, as Grandfather goes off looking for sugar, only to find his cup of tea has been cleared away by the time he gets back.

Ringo's understated style matches the dialogue, as he transforms from bullied loner to master of his own destiny, stopping only to deliver a Nazi salute to the uniformed soldier by the door on his way out. How could anyone in British TV comedy resist such a gesture at the time?

Ringo pauses to take a photograph of his bandmates, before he disappears without explanation. It's like two different genres are meeting at a crossroads: the *nouvelle vague* mood of Ringo's wordless actions, and the Cliff Richard-style musical plot turn. The three remaining Beatles' realisation that Ringo's really left them is reminiscent of Cliff Richard's *The Young Ones*, in which he heads off to rescue his father, leaving his friends bewildered as the clock ticks down to the concert. They head off separately to look for him.

A Taste of Honey

Ringo's parading sequence takes us into French philosophical territory, exploring the existential void that opens up without the gang and the work. The mood of comic melancholy is aided by George Martin's instrumental arrangement of 'This Boy'. Spotted by two girls, who pursue him, Ringo instinctively takes off like a solo version of the film's opening chase. But transformed by a second-hand mac and hat, Fab-ness proves elusive outside of the Four. He can't even sweet-talk a 'Sheila' as Grandfather suggested, and a policeman is taking note.

Producer Bud Ornstein challenged only one scene in Alun Owen's film script. The original version of Ringo's 'going parading' sequence was to show him in the second-hand shop chatting to a 'typical Jewish' proprietor and 'selling a top hat and cutaway coat to East Indian sailors', making them, in Ornstein's opinion, 'look stupid'. However, according to Alexander Walker, the scene Owen wrote to replace it was one of the film's highlights – his encounter with the young truant on the towpath.[25]

On the Thames towpath at Kew, with the industrial chimneys of Brentford in the background, Lester gives us Ringo the Buster Keaton-like lonely soul. We watch him attempting to 'stylishly', as the script puts it, kick a brick down the embankment, but driven in frustration to pull it up and hurl it into the river. In an elegantly timed set-up, the same policeman on his bike rides by just in time to see it happen and call out a rebuke.

'Southerner!' Ringo yells back, before being sideswiped by a rolling car tyre. It's the moment he encounters the Boy.

The energetic David Janson (Jaxon on the film's end credits) was already an experienced stage and screen actor, having spent a year in the cast of the hit stage musical *Oliver!* He arrived with his own clothes, as was standard, and the sequence was shot mostly in order. He didn't know Ringo had turned up hung-over, straight from all-night clubbing.

The first task was to get a take of the car tyre hitting Ringo. Janson recalls: 'It took such a long time for anyone to get the tyre to cooperate till I rolled it.'[26] After multiple attempts by Lester and the crew, Janson on his second attempt got it close enough that Ringo chose to trip over it, and they had the take in the can.

One might assume the sequence was a conscious reference to the social realist style of Tony Richardson's *A Taste of Honey* (1961), in which the troubled heroine, Jo, and her friend Geoffrey are often seen in conversation while walking through the streets and along the canal sides of Salford. However, Janson says the walk and talk emerged through improvisation as they rehearsed. The dialogue crackles with schoolboy war games jargon about being a 'deserter' and words like 'stroppy' and 'wick'. As they attempted to feel their way through the script, Janson noticed Ringo didn't make much eye contact and was instead continually fiddling with his camera. Janson kept his own eyes on the camera as they talked, until Ringo, seeing his keenness, hands it over for him to play with. It rings true as boy and man communicate, unable to look each other in the eye. Lester liked what he saw and got them to repeat it until they had shot the scene. It's a lovely example of how Lester worked with his cast and crew – at speed, but always open to seizing the moment.

Ringo and Janson also filmed some larking around, to make the most of the low tide – throwing stones, Ringo lying on his back, hands folded under his head, looking up at the sky dreaming, without any clue as to his thoughts. Much of the emotional impact of this sequence comes from the editing of Taylor's beautiful images, John Jympson intercutting the play with overlaid dialogue from the walk and talk scene. It gives a sense of hours passing in each other's company, the intimacy of strangers who won't meet again. I have always found this sequence moving, in a way that I can't explain. Janson can: 'I think it was a lot to do with the pace of the scene. The way it was edited and the music – the track is so nice.

Because everything else in the film is quite frenetic … And I think it had a different quality about it.' A kind of opposite time-out to the 'Can't Buy Me Love' runaround.

The idea of one deserter meeting another, and indeed Ringo encountering his younger self, is irresistibly poetic. In real life Ringo had played truant from school and larked around on the south Liverpool banks of the River Mersey, known as the Cast Iron Shore.[27] The Boy is also from a gang of four, each with distinctive personalities. Some fans have even read a match to each Beatle: 'Ginger's mad, he says things all the time' is John; 'Eddy's good at punching and spitting' is strong-willed George; while Paul is supposedly Ding Dong: 'He's a big head and he fancies himself with it, but it's all right because he's one of the gang.' So much is unspoken that we can imagine a Ken Loach version of the Boy's own backstory – where are Social Services? What might he be running away from?

The sequence ends with another Lester touch of happenstance: spotting the upturned single-scull boat and its floundering rower in the Thames. It punctures any sentimentality that might have welled up in the viewer and takes us back into the comedic world of the film.

There is one real shame: the Boy and his gang were to appear together again, outside the Scala Theatre when Grandfather, freshly escaped from the police station, unknowingly enlists their help to outwit the commissionaire to get back inside the theatre. The script states: 'The four little boys from the canal are being driven away by the security guard.' Janson arrived at the Scala Theatre for his second day of filming after another commitment, as arranged, to find Lester had already begun shooting and improvising. With speed of the essence, the small amount of dialogue – 'Six pence. Each. In advance' – was divided up between the three others and Janson watched the shoot, was paid, but was not included in the scene. To throw out that callback seems a rare error of judgement on Lester's part.

Ringo's parading continues at the Turk's Head pub, close to Twickenham Studios, as he tackles a stale pub sandwich and soon finds himself stared at in silence by the regulars like a stranger in a

The bearded man is Bob Godfrey

Western walking into a saloon. The landlady's steely call, 'On your way', I recognised as a British TV colloquialism of pub landlording. As a child I found this scene not comic, but almost traumatic. It chimed with a more visceral social anxiety – of being marked as an outsider, something the schoolchild and the immigrant have in common with Ringo the underdog. It would have helped if I'd known then that the solemn-faced customers were Lester's comedy collaborators, including the creator of the children's cartoon series *Roobarb and Custard* (1974; 2005), animator Bob Godfrey.

A deleted scene in which Paul meets an actress (Isla Blair) originally followed here (see Chapter 4) but in the released version, we are back inside the studio, where Grandfather has confessed all to a distraught Norm and the director, watching the clock tick down to the final run-through. John, Paul and George return from their fruitless hunt for Ringo, and the plotlines start to merge: Grandfather, trying to hawk his forged autographed photos to the waiting crowd of children, is taken away by the police. He's soon to be joined by Ringo, whose would-be chivalry on a building site (the last scene to be shot in the film) goes awry in pure silent film mode.

Ringo at the police station, with Deryck Guyler on the left

At the police station we hear the only dialogue that has genuinely dated in the entire film, when the constable and sergeant discuss Ringo's alleged misdemeanours:

Ah, a little savage is he?
Yeah. A proper little aborigine.

That apart, the scene has a nostalgic sweetness, partly thanks to the avuncular presence of TV stalwart Deryck Guyler, and particularly through the contrast with Grandfather, drawing on cultural memories of British colonial brutality in Ireland, only to have a kindly Irish constable run after him to return his photographs.

As a warm-up to the elaborate slapstick chase sequence about to start, we are back in the control booth, with George drawing a moustache and glasses on the face of Norm on the TV monitor. It's a riff on a similar gag Lester filmed in 1956 for *A Show Called Fred*, with Graham Stark speaking to camera while noughts and crosses are drawn on his face.

David Janson watched this scene shot without him

A light jazz version of the song 'A Hard Day's Night' strikes up as Grandfather attempts his assault on the theatre – police out front – and is the scene that originally featured the Boy from the riverside. Its whole tone, with that jazzy accompaniment and the bucket-over-head jape to get past the doorman, reminds me very much of a Cliff Richard film. Lester disguises that obvious similarity by making the audience watch Grandfather's explanation through a camera monitor on the studio floor, and having John, Paul and George run off barking and hooting, leaving the forlorn director alone in his torment.

Grandfather's failed attempt to convince the uniformed commissionaire that he's Paul's grandfather had a bizarre real-life parallel. John's estranged father, Fred, turned up at the Scala during shooting. He hadn't seen John since childhood. Associate producer Denis O'Dell recalled in 2002:

You can imagine Freddie trying to make his way to the front of five hundred people outside the Scala Theatre who are pressing to get in, and my production manager's trying to keep them out and he's saying, 'But I'm John Lennon's father!'

Informed about the unexpected visitor, John said to Dell: 'Tell him to fuck off.' They eventually let him in, and father and son had a brief conversation.[28]

One wonders about the impact on John, especially when later he lectures Paul's grandfather about how he took a wrong turn and should have gone to America and become a senior citizen of Boston. Instead, 'you're a lonely old man from Liverpool'.

But first there is Lester's Buster Keaton tribute in the elaborate silent film-style police chase sequence, shot around the streets of Notting Hill in west London. Apparently modelled on *Cops* (1922), Lester mimicked the way Keaton framed his chases using the camera as an additional proscenium arch. We see this repeatedly as they run in and out of the police station (really a school) and out of Charlotte Mews, with – a lovely moment this – a little old lady in the dress shop window to the right of the frame getting in position to catch them go by. It's intercut with a running gag about a car thief, given to actor John Bluthal, who would return in *Help!* as the chief henchman of the murderous Indian death cult. The Victorian church behind was not a bombsite, but was captured in the middle of demolition; an incidental sign of the rapid demographic change in London at

the time, alongside an equally rapid ongoing decline in traditional Anglican church attendance.

The slapstick chase becomes emblematic of the Swinging Sixties, as well as generating another pop video template (think Supergrass's 'Alright' [1995] and almost every *Monkees*' TV show episode). The exception to the many poor copycat films (*The Mini-Mob* aka *The Mini-Affair* [1967], for example) is the satire *Smashing Time* (1967), which, though misunderstood on release, shares Lester's love of old Hollywood slapstick, and particularly embraces the custard pie fight to mock the self-importance of London's 'cool' scene.

There is, though, a moment of emotional pause. Once the chase is done, against a stylish shot of the boys milling around, changing jackets by a coat rack, Paul speaks with quiet contempt for Grandfather's shenanigans. And John delivers his thoughtful put-down with a smile that addresses every old codger moaning about the young. Loose threads tied up, the show must go on!

Lester's multi-camera shoot of the concert reaped huge dividends. He had six cameras filming simultaneously with 10:1 zoom lenses. According to Gilbert Taylor, a lull in the UK film industry at the time meant 'we were able to engage crack operators on every one of them and give them orders to shoot and shoot and shoot'.[29] With all the screaming in the auditorium it was impossible to hear each other or issue instructions, so the camera crew were given free rein to film what grabbed them. The concert sequence's impact was achieved in its editing, which was Lester's favourite part of film-making. He chose to include many of the quick blurred pans across the theatre, which were not purposely filmed but the result of camera operators rushing to capture an interesting moment elsewhere.

Elaine Jensen, then fourteen, was one of many children recruited through industry contacts and stage schools to be in the 350-strong audience. Future pop stars Phil Collins and Linda Lewis were also there. Twelve-year-old Lynn Wake got in thanks to her aunt, who worked with the wife of the casting director. They arrived from around 9 am and filmed until late into the afternoon, with the instruction, before shooting began, to shout and scream as the Beatles mimed to playback. The enthusiasm captured on camera for the most part came very naturally.

After a free packed lunch, filming resumed. By then, Elaine recalls, 'our throats were very sore from constant screaming'.[30] So much so that a man with a rolled-up newspaper was assigned to stand to the side of the stage to whoop them up. 'He would wave it around and around in circles, and the faster he went, the more enthusiastically we had to scream.' Lynn – who gets a screaming close-up at the climax of 'She Loves You' – was moved to the front of the stalls at one point and recalls John asking her if she was all right. She went home hoarse, with a headache, but happy and £3 17s. and 6d. the richer.[31]

Viewers experience a revelatory closeness to the band in performance, sweat glowing on their skin. Careful viewing reveals how Lester did not fill the theatre to the rafters, but rather managed a fixed number of children, moving them in blocks into different seating areas, with the rest shrouded in darkness.

Empty stalls as the fans were moved to fill the balcony (photograph by Bert Cann)

By 'I Should Have Known Better', the sound mix starts to raise the volume on the screaming. The focus is switching from the performance to the girls leaning over the balconies. The cameras spin across the faces – matching the chaos and hysteria. There are tears from the girl in the sailor dress, while a boy covers his ears to scream even as the sound deafens him.

At this point the music stops, and the screaming is allowed to rage undipped – an echo of the crowd at the station so long ago in our journey with this band. The climax – in every sense of the word – is close. By the time 'She Loves You' begins, the balance has shifted, and the fans have taken over the film.

My favourite fan shot in the concert sequence is a zoom-in on an elegant young South Asian woman with a 1960s bob and a white

dress standing up in delight. (She appears again later, upstairs on
a balcony edge – evidence of how Lester moved the crowd around
the auditorium.) Behind her, we see two young boys of colour – one
Asian, shy with his school blazer badge visible, one mixed race – right
at the heart of the crowd. Given the reality of segregation in the US,
which the Beatles challenged when they toured there, the shot has an
understated power. The Beatles were loved by everyone, and Britain,
for all its complicated social tensions, is captured in this film as
having a multiracial reality.

The head shaking and rocking – resembling a religious revival –
becomes more frenzied, even as the camerawork finds moments of
humour – a girl stopping to swallow or take a breath before her next
scream, or girls hugging each other in shared best-friend bliss. In
the final moments of 'She Loves You', Jympson edits a young girl's
rattling headshake to the exact rat-tat-tat gunfire intonation of the
final 'With a love like that ...'

'BEATLES' suddenly appears on the lightboard behind them –
the second and last appearance of their name in the entire picture.
The screaming is allowed to swell as the band take their bows. The
final shots of the crowd offer us some more glimpses of the reality

of 1960s youth: a boy in a sensible cardigan and tie, like a miniature version of his dad, next to an older teen dressed in full mod style with a sharply folded handkerchief in his jacket pocket.

We cut to Spinetti – head bowed in exhaustion – collapsed over the mixing desk, his assistant removing the director's headphones to deliver a calming head massage.

After the day's filming, cameraman Paul Wilson had to visit the dentist, in terrible pain from the vibrations rattling the amalgam in his fillings: 'It was absolute agony, it really was',[32] while Gilbert Taylor was so horrified by the hysteria that he chose not to work on the follow-up Beatles film: 'I really disapproved of the effect they were having when I witnessed the hysteria our multiple cameras recorded.'[33]

Aftermath

After the concert, the band exit the stage, followed by the showgirls and costumed singers and actors we'd met earlier. It is a very faint reminder of the idea that the Beatles were supposedly performing as part of a longer TV variety show. And then Norm delivers the news that they're heading off straight to Wolverhampton for a 'midnight matinee'. The existential hell of their lives enters another cycle. We realise the film could have started here. It could be an episode of *Black Mirror* (2011–) were it not for the smiles that erupt as Norm and John's stand-off turns to camaraderie, witnessed by Paul. Who runs the mysterious 'office' issuing updated instructions, of which Norm is only a minion?

The war is still raging, though, and RAF cameraman Gilbert Taylor captures them heading on to their next mission, the title song reprising, as they race out – day for night – into a helicopter rather than a train, and away. The photographs Paul grabs off Grandfather and throws out as they take off are a final scattering of the ashes of the dead, a static image they left behind long ago.

2 Making *A Hard Day's Night*

Eighty per cent work and twenty per cent was all laffs.

Ringo Starr[34]

The Beatles had already made their mark on British TV shows such as ITV's *Thank Your Lucky Stars* (1961–6), but the American film company United Artists was driven by the fact that the band were selling records and had a huge and growing youth following.

People had made films including British pop acts before. Most were cheap cash-ins, shoehorning in performances in the background to the main action. The Beatles, who had gone to see many of these films for a glimpse of performers they admired, had in 1963 turned down at least five offers to make one.[35] As George explained,

They wanted us to just be the group in the back or just pass through a film; just sing a couple of songs. But we didn't want that because we've never enjoyed that sort of film. So we waited until we had a reasonable offer.[36]

Some of the pop films toyed with the real stories behind artist success, but through the viewfinder of sensationalism. In Val Guest's *Expresso Bongo* (1959), based on a West End musical, Cliff Richard plays 'Bongo Herbert', discovered performing in a Soho coffee bar. It was a reference to a real place – the 2i's on Old Compton Street – which had opened in 1956 and was the ground zero of that first generation of home-grown British pop stars such as Cliff Richard and Tommy Steele, who played there. Harry is exploited by Laurence Harvey's seedy Fagin-esque Soho agent, and sexually preyed upon, too, by an older woman. The film was X-rated by the BBFC, as was Edmond T. Gréville's *Beat Girl* (1960), starring Adam Faith. The latter was even more overtly moral panic cinema, about the impact of this new coffee bar culture on a middle-class teenage girl. Its US title was *Wild for Kicks*.

A year later Val Guest made a journalistic science-fiction horror about a nuclear-test disaster. As part of its contemporary realism, *The Day the Earth Caught Fire* (1961) featured a trad jazz apocalypse as the hero and heroine tried to fight their way through hordes of young people, awaiting the end of the world, engaged in a nihilistic orgy of skimpy outfits and trombones. Pop culture itself was portrayed as an alien horror in our midst – the viewpoint being the gaze of baffled middle-aged men.

By contrast, the man who would direct *AHDN* had made a trad jazz music film whose very title seems a deliberate riposte to *Wild for Kicks*. *It's Trad, Dad!* was, like its director Richard Lester, very much on the side of the kids. His film was about trad jazz-loving teenagers who challenge the mean old council officials' attempt to ban the music at their beloved coffee bar. It was Lester's first feature film and he described it himself as a 'pop quickie. It makes *A Hard Day's Night* seem like a work of Jean-Paul Sartre.'[37]

Born in 1932 in Philadelphia, Lester had studied psychology at university but dropped out, horrified at how students, training to be psychologists, were encouraged to institutionalise children too quickly, based on fixed tests. Instead he resolved to be a TV director by twenty, working his way up the ranks from stagehand to film director by thirty (he did it with two months to spare). Although a decade older than the Beatles, he had formed his approach to directing in his own equivalent to their 'ten thousand hours' of practice, as famously hypothesised by Malcolm Gladwell in his book *Outliers* (2008). Aged twenty-one, Lester had been given a week's holiday as a reward for directing 260 live TV shows in a year.[38] By 1956, he had moved to Britain and was directing groundbreaking comedy shows for ITV London franchise Associated-Rediffusion, as well as dozens of TV ads. From ad directing he learned all the tricks to make an impact, having the money to experiment with techniques such as editing, playing with sound, slow motion and undercranking.[39] His 1961 'Lunch Date' ad for Nimble bread is a single swooping take of a young woman running down a crowded staircase and leaping into the arms of her beau. It looks like the perfect *nouvelle vague* seventeen-second audition tape for *AHDN*.[40]

The term Beatlemania, as a description of the fan hysteria that surrounded the band, was first recorded in print on 13 October 1963 in the *Observer* newspaper. That month, fresh from their third number one single, the orgiastic 'She Loves You', the Beatles appeared on the nation's flagship variety TV show, *Sunday Night at the London Palladium* (1955–74) – 'for most British entertainers a pinnacle career achievement'.[41] It was just such a TV variety show that became the template for the live TV show at the heart of the *AHDN* film script. The press and broadcasters couldn't get enough of these four handsome and charming young northern men, who delivered music and wit with such confidence.

Noel Rogers, the head of United Artists Music in the UK, suggested the idea of a film to the movie arm of UA, and to Dick James, whose Dick James Music owned half of Northern Songs. (Publishing rights in the Lennon–McCartney songs were held by Northern Songs.) James discussed it with Brian Epstein, and the message came back that the band were open to an offer. That offer would quickly get approved by head office in the US, thanks to a short chain of command and, in the words of Mark Lewisohn, 'a handful of creative film businessmen to say yes or no'.[42]

So it was that in October 1963 Bud Ornstein of United Artists asked 45-year-old Walter Shenson if he could make a film with the Beatles. *Beatlemania* became its working title. 'You mean those young men with the long hair and the guitars?' recalled Shenson later. 'They said "just make sure there are enough new songs by the Beatles for an album and don't go over budget."'[43]

Lester had heard about the Beatles from friends who'd been to the Cavern, and he had directed *The Mouse That Roared* sequel, *The Mouse on the Moon* (1963), for Shenson. When he approached Shenson about a possible new project together and learned of the

Beatles film idea, Lester, in Shenson's rather fanciful-sounding recall, 'jumped on the chair in the Hilton Hotel coffee shop and said, "My God, can I direct it?"'. Lester went off, bought their debut album and started coming up with ideas. He described his approach to the film as: 'Essentially adapting the best bits of the French nouvelle vague into something which had a very earthy and English quality about it.'[44] Lester felt strongly that he was in sync with young cinemagoers. He later said he had 'that sense that my metabolic rate and the audience's were close enough that I didn't have to question it'.[45] The next step was to get the Beatles on board.

After approaching Brian Epstein, Shenson arranged to meet the band, and, when they failed to turn up to the appointment, Epstein took Shenson to their Mayfair flat and they all crammed into the back of a London taxi. It was, said Shenson, like being 'in the middle of a Marx Brothers comedy, because the boys were very funny'.[46] 'Every time we came to a Stop sign one of them jumped out and bought a newspaper which had Beatles headlines.'[47] Shenson suggested Lester to direct, mentioning his work with the Goons, which the Beatles loved, and they liked the idea very much. As schoolboys they'd watched Lester's two ITV series, *A Show Called Fred* and *Son of Fred*, and particularly loved his *The Running, Jumping & Standing Still Film*, which had run on continuous repeat at the Tatler News Theatre cinema in Liverpool. On at least one occasion in 1961, the pre-Ringo Beatles went there to watch it after playing a Cavern lunchtime gig.[48]

This meeting of minds would yield huge rewards on screen. Like the Beatles, who had benefitted from the end of compulsory National Service, Lester had a strong spirit of anti-deference. As he later recalled:

I think that Suez was a defining moment. That episode of dishonesty and collusion among government that we thought were proper, provoked – not only in me, but in a massive number of people in this country – a sense of Let's Get Out of Here![49]

Walter Shenson and Richard Lester with the Beatles (photograph by Bert Cann)

Lester noticed that, unlike any other very famous people he'd met before, the band were very self-aware and had an ironic sense of detachment from their own celebrity, often wryly ribbing the inane questions and fuddy-duddy tone of their press and broadcast interrogators.

Shenson's Proscenium Films agreed contracts with Northern Songs for the required number of songs by Lennon and McCartney, and with Epstein's NEMS Enterprises for the Beatles' appearance. The Nems deal for one film, with the option on two more, was for £25,000 ($70,000), with 10 per cent of the net profits. Percentage-wise, more than Epstein had initially considered, but less than United Artists had been prepared to agree. 'A fair, if unspectacular deal', according to Lewisohn,[50] who says it was later renegotiated in 1964 to £25,000 plus 25 per cent of net profits, to be paid into a new film company, Subafilms.

The film was to be shot in black and white with a budget of £200,000 ($560,000). The original plan was to shoot for six consecutive weeks from February 1964, with a July release, which would maximise ticket sales in the school holidays. But when Epstein secured a deal with Ed Sullivan to feature the band on his show on two consecutive weeks in February, the dates for the film shoot got pushed back to March.

Lester's first encounter with the Beatles on 16 October 1963 laid out for him the essential heart of the film they would make together, and the key character of Victor Spinetti's harried TV director. Lester arrived to find chaos and a huge crowd of fans of all ages and journalists at the Playhouse Theatre in London, where the band were due to rehearse and record a BBC radio show. But they were running late. He saw how they coped with the madness good-naturedly, taking it all in their stride, in contrast to the BBC producer who was 'tearing his hair out at all the delays and distractions'.[51]

'Having met them, the die is automatically cast,' said Lester years later. 'You're enthralled, and it was over from that time on. That's all I really wanted to do – was to make that film – because I felt there was something marvellous in them and in their music.'[52]

For screenwriter, Lester had originally wanted TV writer Johnny Speight, future creator of the controversial sitcom *Till Death Us Do Part* (1966–75), which spawned the US version *All in the Family* (1971–9) and would feature a grumpy old man at its heart (Alf Garnett/Archie Bunker). Or possibly Galton and Simpson, creators of *Steptoe and Son* and *Hancock's Half Hour* (1956–60).[53] But Lester had already worked with Alun Owen, the Beatles' choice, back in 1955 on his own one-off British TV programme, *The Dick Lester Show*, which, in the words of Mark Lewisohn, 'if not actually funny, was comically experimental'.[54]

Alun Owen, a Liverpudlian of Welsh heritage, had already been approached by Epstein about writing a script, on the suggestion of the band, back in September. John and Paul had enjoyed his TV play *No Trams to Lime Street* (1959) and had started writing a kitchen sink drama of their own as teenagers, called *Pilchard* – four pages of it inspired by his style.[55] Owen was paid £8,200 for his script. Dispatched to see the band in Dublin, he came up with the concept of them as prisoners of their own success.

The decision to film in black and white may have been budgetary from United Artists' point of view, but it fitted with the Beatles' self-image. The black-and-white cover of their second album, *With the Beatles*, released at the end of November 1963, captured the zeitgeist. Defying EMI's concern, they had decided to stick with Robert Freeman's chic Expressionist shadowed portraits, like four heavenly bodies in partial eclipse – an elegant riposte to the silly cut-out heads that were standard for pop records and posters at the time. The band themselves, with their mostly grammar school and art college background, weren't afraid of being arthouse. As Paul said in 2002: 'We were really glad it was a black-and-white film … It just seemed harder, more student-y … That's a bad word, but you know what I mean. More artsy. We liked all that stuff.'[56] Walter Shenson highlighted this aesthetic as a marketing line in an early promotional interview, telling the *Daily Mail*: 'It's going to be a far-out story. And it will be in black and white because the Beatles are black and white people.'[57]

Nineteen sixty-four arrived. From 16 January they began a three-week residency at the Olympia in Paris, wrote many of the songs for the film in their hotel suite at the George V, with the aid of a piano brought in specially, and learned they'd got their first US number one single ('I Want to Hold Your Hand'). It was there that Lester and Owen witnessed the band larking around under siege and hiding when they'd been naughty, which crystallised into the final screenplay. George Martin went round after they failed to turn up to a recording session: 'As soon as I entered, they exploded in all directions; they ran behind couches and chairs and one put a lampshade over his head. Then from behind the sofa and chairs came a chorus of, "Sorry George, sorry George, sorry George …"'[58] Still images, such as Harry Benson's famous photo for the *Daily Express* of the boys having a pillow fight in their suite, already captured them in motion. Imagine capturing them in moving pictures!

Then, on 7 February, it was off to New York for *The Ed Sullivan Show* (1948–71) and their first American appearances, where much of the imagery of the film got its real-life early run in TV documentary and news broadcast footage: their witty press conferences, the band holed up in their hotel room wanting to sneak off for adventures, the young fans chasing them down the streets and screaming through their concerts. A semi-staged version of all of this would be the essence of *AHDN*.

Three days after they returned from the US, on 25 February – George Harrison's twenty-first birthday – the Beatles were in the studio to begin recording some of the songs for the film. They had written five of the seven contractually required in Paris and Miami, and then recorded nine songs in total in four days at EMI Studios on London's Abbey Road. The very next day, Monday 2 March, they began seven weeks of filming, completing on 24 April.

Denis O'Dell, brought in as associate producer to liaise between the creative and the money sides, said it was his suggestion to film the train sequences on a real moving train, instead of using back projection in a studio, as was the norm.[59] British Rail provided the specially chartered train, with carriages adapted to accommodate dolly tracks and electrical generators, and the Beatles and crew convened each day, initially at Paddington, to travel back and forth to Minehead in Somerset and later to Newton Abbot in Devon. They clocked up 2,500 miles over six days of filming. Each evening the Beatles would leave the train early at a suburban stop to avoid the awaiting crowds.

The band took a few days to recognise they'd need to adjust their night owl lifestyle, once the reality of early 6 am starts kicked in. For the first week, according to George, 'We couldn't get the hang of it, so were still going out at night and getting up in the morning.'[60]

The film was shot mostly in chronological order, with the on-board train sequences in the first week, which helped too, though the band were rather harsh about their early performance: 'There's bits that make us curl up in that film,' said George. John recalled: 'The first we did was the train – we're all dead nervous, you can see us. Practically the whole of the train bit we're just going to pieces; just so embarrassed about it all.'

'Eighty per cent work and twenty per cent was all laffs,' observed Ringo in a press interview in July 1964. And the combination paid off. As Paul observed: 'Even when we were very tired and really knocked out and we'd do a thing, when we actually saw it on a screen it looked quite funny.'[61] Photographer David Hurn, who played Monopoly with the band during the shoot, was struck by their screen power: 'They weren't actors and they didn't have to be. It is why the film works.'[62]

Perhaps the epitome of this is the sequence where Ringo leaves the band to find himself. Dialogue with the young boy he encounters on the Thames towpath was cut back to a minimum, because of Ringo's hangover. But, as a result, the sequence has the melancholic, understated atmosphere of a British social realist drama. It is surely to Lester's as well as Ringo's credit that reviews singled out Ringo's naturalistic acting in this scene as a revelation – a highlight of the film. You wha? Indeed.

Every surviving still or film of on-location footage shows Richard Lester either smiling in delight or engaged with passion. He has said that making TV ads was like hitting tennis backhands against a wall.[63] Vital practice for the real effort of a tournament. And the seven-week shoot of *AHDN* was quite the tournament.

He didn't use a shot list but ad-libbed depending on what he found, and trusted his DOP. He found ways to troubleshoot a path through the mayhem of the crowds who appeared everywhere they were filming. Though they had hired extras to play fans, many more fans would turn up having heard about the film. On one occasion, that meant scrapping an exterior London street shoot when it was besieged by screaming fans, and setting up the press conference sequence indoors, with a combination of extras and real journalists who'd arrived on location looking for a story.

Lester negotiating the challenge of filming the Beatles on the streets of London
(photograph by Bert Cann)

For the famous 360-degree pan around Paul McCartney in the
'And I Love Her' sequence, Lester remembers they 'rigged up a child's
swing, dropped it from the ceiling, put the camera on it and walked
this child's swing around Paul'. Lester didn't have a director's chair.
He was on his feet like the Beatles themselves, hoofing it.

Lester was already filming even before the official start of the
shoot. He saw the band being chased as they were about to board the
train for the first day's shoot:

I shouted to the camera operator, 'give me the camera', and he handed it
to me and I stuck it out the window as they were running to get on the
train to get away from a real crowd to get on to do their first day's shooting.
I didn't care that we get everything right. What I wanted to do was to catch
the moment.

Continuity supervisor Rita Davison wrote:

First shot taken while I was in the ladies' toilet. I've no idea who was in it. I think they were the Beatles. But they were wearing the clothing they came in, not what was supposed to be worn. It was photographed by the director. I trust this is not the way we intend to go on. God help me.

Lester recalls: 'Well it was the way the film went on and she did stay to the end and she was a very nice woman.'

Half of the first day's shooting negatives were lost after the return to Paddington, when a young clapper loader with Beatle-like hair panicked as the screaming started and tried to outrun the fans, dropping the canisters, which fell open, exposing the film.

Even photographer Hurn, who'd covered the 1956 Hungarian uprising, was disturbed by the ferocity of the fan hysteria. And it wasn't just the teenagers. David Janson saw how, after the Beatles finished a press conference during filming, adults descended like flies to snatch as souvenirs anything the four had touched: cigarette ends, ashtrays, pieces of paper.

When Walter Shenson got home after viewing what had survived of the first day's rushes, his wife asked him how it went. 'I really can't tell,' he said. 'All I know is I couldn't keep my eyes off the screen.'

The band usually had weekends off. From Tuesday 10 March the Beatles spent two weeks filming mostly in or near Twickenham Studios, with excursions to Gatwick airport on Friday the 13th for their helicopter shots, and to Les Ambassadeurs on 17 March for the casino sequence.[64]

A photograph with the Labour Party leader Harold Wilson at the Variety Club lunch on 19 March captured the sense that the Beatles were election gold. Wilson presented them with their trophies as Showbusiness Personalities of 1963 and basked in the aura of being a party leader who was on the side of young voters. It was a striking contrast with the future Conservative Party leader,

Ted Heath, then Lord Privy Seal, who the previous year had said he found it hard to recognise the way the Beatles spoke as the Queen's English, and been mocked in return by John in an ITN news interview. 'We're not going to vote for Ted,' declared John with a hard stare to camera.[65] Seven months after the Variety Club photograph was taken, Wilson became prime minister, ending thirteen years of Conservative rule.

From 23 March, the location for the next seven days was the Scala Theatre in Charlotte Street, with the concert finale filmed there on 31 March and the press conference on the last day – 2 April.

The famous opening train station sequences weren't filmed until 5 and 12 April – on two consecutive Sundays at Marylebone station, when trains were not running.[66] Ringo's towpath scenes were filmed on Thursday 9 April at Kew, with George's solo encounter with the ad agency executive filmed on the 13th. A deleted sequence in which the band are stuck in a traffic jam was shot on Tuesday the 14th in St Margarets, close to the Twickenham Studios, and on Thursday the 16th they shot the Buster Keaton-esque police chase sequence around Notting Hill.

In the final week Lester efficiently swept up all he still needed: on Friday 17 April he filmed the boys nightclubbing in the Garrison Room. On Saturday the 18th they did essential post-sync dubbing on their dialogue at Twickenham Studios, while on Monday the 20th and Tuesday the 21st Paul filmed his solo scene with actress Isla Blair. Shooting on Wednesday and Thursday captured the two crucial locations of larking around for the 'Can't Buy Me Love' sequence, but also more of the police chase, featuring the car thief. Then, on Friday the 24th – the last morning of filming – the final shots, of Ringo's disastrous Sir Walter Raleigh act, were filmed on a building site in West Ealing. The Beatles attended the cast wrap party that afternoon at a hall behind the Turk's Head pub.

Remarkably, during this time, the band were still making many other radio, TV and live concert appearances, including rehearsals for a Rediffusion special, *Around the Beatles* (1964), directed by

Rita Gillespie and produced by Jack Good, who had together created the landmark pop music TV show *Oh Boy!* (1958–9). The programme included a performance by the boys of a scene from Shakespeare's *A Midsummer Night's Dream* in Elizabethan costume, surrounded by adoring fans.

Two other songs, including the title track, were written and recorded during filming and post-production. Ringo, whose verbal Ringo-isms often delighted his bandmates, had coined the phrase 'a hard day's night' around 1963. It appears in John's book *In His Own Write*, published during filming in March 1964. After a few weeks of being bantered around, it was adopted as the title and announced to the press on 17 April. Shenson recalls telling John about the opening sequence and that

We need a nice fast song to start the picture. John Lennon said, 'what about the lyrics?' I said, 'a hard day's night till I come home to you'. He said, 'that's terrible'. I said, 'that's why you're the songwriter and I'm not'. The following morning at 8 o'clock Paul and John summoned me to their dressing room. They were sitting there with guitars at the ready … And they sang and played A *Hard Day's Night* for me. And remember I'd just asked for this the night before.[67]

The lyrics were written on a birthday card featuring a picture of a boy driving a steam train, sent to John's son, Julian, who had just turned one.[68]

The level of soundtrack album pre-orders in the US meant the film was in profit even before it opened. After the success of the film, Shenson chose to give Lester 1 per cent of the net profits. Otherwise his fee would have been a straight £6,000.[69]

Wilfrid Brambell, Norman Rossington and John Junkin were the only other cast members with such an all-inclusive deal, with Brambell paid £4,500, three times the fee of Rossington on £1,500, and Junkin on £900. Victor Spinetti, was, like the rest of the cast, on a day rate. He was paid £525 for seven days' work at £75 per day. Kenneth Haigh and Isla Blair as the young actress in the eventually deleted scene were both paid the same £100 day rate, while David Janson was paid a £25 day rate – the same as the bit-part actors.[70]

From his extensive work in TV comedy, Lester had a rich contacts book of stage and screen talent to draw on in casting his film. Wilfrid Brambell was a pragmatic choice, a high-profile TV star of a hit sitcom. Spinetti had appeared in Joan Littlewood's groundbreaking war satire *Oh! What a Lovely War* on the London stage. *AHDN* is sprinkled with contemporary comedy stalwarts in little cameos: Derek Nimmo (fellow alumnus of John's old school, Quarry Bank) as the stage magician and the Tony award-winning Anna Quayle as the theatrical luvvie. But Lester also dropped in touches of contemporary cultural glamour that the cinema audience would have spotted, notably the striking Rosemarie Frankland (Miss World 1961) as a featured showgirl.

Key to the production was Lester's understanding of how to capture the best of the Beatles. Interestingly, the Maysles brothers' footage seen in *Beatles '64* documents many of the situations that were written into the final film, though it should be noted that Denis O'Dell has no memory of watching the original Granada documentary, which aired on 12 February 1964 at 10.25 pm, by which time the main script would have been mostly finished.[71]

Granada's film, titled *Yeah! Yeah! Yeah! The Beatles in New York* (1964), based on three days of rushes, showed similar scenes to *AHDN* of their desire for escape. They do make it to a nightclub, where Ringo dances with abandon with two very cool NY girls, besieged at every turn by enthusiastic hordes of passionate, mostly female fans. Even the V-patterned sweater Spinetti's director wears is, by pure coincidence, similar to the one worn by the rather sad, middle-aged DJ Murray the K – who we see in his radio cubicle. Spinetti's director, to his credit, doesn't pretend to be one of the kids.

The most significant difference is how naturally in the documentary footage the Beatles engaged directly with the cameras and larked about for them in the real world, including at their very first press conference, just as they had done on British entertainment shows for the past two years. 'Not you again,' says George to the camera as they board their flight back to London. They soon start lending a hand, each of them at different times calling out and marking a fresh numbered 'take'. In contrast to his more limited persona in *AHDN*, Paul plays up to the camera with the greatest confidence, goading the operator to be daring, or putting on a Yorkshire accent to joke about listening to himself on 't'radio'.

I wonder if part of their nervousness on the film shoot was the challenge of having to avoid looking at and playing to the camera. Except, of course, in that 'Can't Buy Me Love' breakout scene. While it might have been because of time pressures, given the production's quick turnaround, Lester's decision to individually hard-mic the Beatles – with the cables hidden down their shirts – was counterintuitively smart. It may have limited their movement, but he captured their real voices as they delivered their lines in the moment and minimised the need for the then common artifice of post-sync dubbing, when dialogue is re-recorded much later in a sound studio and overlaid on the footage. It kept everything fresh, including, as far as possible, their natural ad-libs. It also made it easier, after the film was complete, to dismiss any suggestion of dubbing over their natural Scouse accents.[72]

Lester's habit of filming rehearsals to capture spontaneity worked well with the Beatles' natural riffing sensibility and for actors like Janson and Spinetti. There were frustrations, though. Ringo remembered Brambell, as a professional actor, stopping dead as soon as the scripted scene was done, meaning many of the Beatles' ad-libs did not develop and they lost the natural ends of scenes when the four of them would be going off in different directions. John felt the spontaneity and humour of his quips were too often diminished by repeated takes. 'You ad lib something quite good and everybody laughs, the technicians laugh, and the next minute you're told to "take it again", so your "ad lib" gets drier and drier until it doesn't sound funny anymore.'[73]

But overall, they could concentrate on just being themselves. Owen's script was written in short exchanges, so they could learn the lines in little bursts on the day, just before delivery. The deleted scenes reveal where Owen's script was overwritten. Between the bathroom scene and their arrival at the theatre was a sequence, featuring actor Frank Thornton and focused on John, when the band are stuck in a traffic jam in their chauffeur-driven car. Owen's dialogue had John play-acting a Western, complete with a fantasy shooting of bullets, as in *Billy Liar*, at a snooty male executive in the car ahead.

Most of the film's soundtrack album had been recorded before filming began but the title song came later – recorded on 16 April, after a long day filming the police chase. It featured that opening crashing guitar chord – the G eleventh suspended fourth.[74] The jangling arpeggios on the fade-out would also form a beautiful part of the opening sequence as the train pulled out of the station. This would all be tied up in the editing, where the energy of *AHDN* would be bottled.

Lester had only a few weeks to put it together, but with the skill of John Jympson, careful logging by assistant editor Pamela Tomling of all those multi-camera shoots of the concert sequences, and some firm decisions to jettison entire scenes and one of the songs, 'You Can't Do That', from the concert, the film came in at a pacy eighty-seven minutes. Just in time to be shown to its Hollywood backers ahead of its premiere on 6 July.

3 *A Hard Day's Night* and TV

It's a young man's medium. I just can't take the pace.

Victor Spinetti as the director in *AHDN*

Writing in 2025, as live television viewing seems to be retreating into obsolescence, it can be hard to appreciate the power of TV as the vital cultural force it was, both for the Beatles' career and in society at large. By February 1964, when the Beatles returned home from their first US trip, so great was mainstream interest that the BBC included footage of the band's arrival on *Grandstand* (1958–2007), their Saturday afternoon sports strand.[75] A significant part of the charm of *AHDN* is as a period snapshot of the interplay between old and new cultures through the box in the living room. In 1964, nine years after the launch of the new commercial channel ITV, British television offered new experimental plays and drama series, live discussion shows, sitcoms such *Steptoe and Son* and, of course, pop music shows for the newly emergent teenage generation. *Top of the Pops* (1964–2006) joined ITV's *Ready, Steady, Go!* (1963–6) on the airwaves. There was even a whole new channel – the often highbrow BBC2, launched in April 1964 – to offer more niche programming.

When Richard Lester came to the UK, he also started working in commercials, and was one of a cohort of bright young directors including Clive Donner (*Nothing But the Best*) and John Schlesinger (*Billy Liar*), bringing advertising energy to their feature-film work. The short comedy sketches he directed with the Goons and on Spike Milligan's *A Show Called Fred* and *Son of Fred* often broke the fourth wall, revealing the corridors and cameras of the TV sets, and laughing studio staff, undermining the patronising tone of much TV presentation, and instead welcoming the audience as equals into the process.

Making about fifteen shows a week for American television, Lester had also witnessed the bizarre accidents and mishaps that occurred in live TV, with its formulaic drama plots and relentless ad spots. Lester found his characteristic surrealism in such comedic incidents, 'like the dog that went mad in the studio and ripped down the set, revealing another one behind it, so that our actors who were in eighteenth-century costumes suddenly found themselves part of a 1944 prisoner-of-war camp'.[76] Grandfather's appearance through a trapdoor during a rehearsal of a Strauss operetta is very much a 'happening' in that spirit.

The TV studio programmes being rehearsed in *AHDN* are themselves a fascinating glimpse into the mid-1960s world of TV entertainment and Lester's celebration of its bizarre juxtapositions. As well as the opera scene, we glimpse multiple showgirl dance troupes, and, thanks to the extras in the canteen working on other TV shows, an eighteenth-century costume drama and another featuring World War II German soldiers – that perennial subject of postwar British drama. Sharing an anti-institutional attitude with Spike Milligan, Lester's work with the Goons and on later films, including *Help!* and *How I Won the War* (1967), would often mock the military and its hierarchy.

All broadcasters at the time, as documented by such archive specialists as the curators of the BFI's Missing Believed Wiped strand, chose too often to discard or wipe tapes of pop music and popular shows such as *Doctor Who*, in favour of retaining recordings of highbrow art forms. The Strauss operetta would have been more likely to survive than the Beatles. Many of the Beatles' early appearances on British TV were deleted in this way. For example, their first BBC TV appearance, on *The 625 Show* (1963) in April 1963, was erased by the BBC's Engineering department as late as January 1967, as part of its routine wiping of tapes for reuse.[77] Lester himself was saddened to realise in later years that out-takes and deleted scenes from both *AHDN* and *Help!* had been ruthlessly discarded from the studios' film archives. The survival of the film concert performance of 'You Can't Do That', dropped from the final edit, was thanks to a copy being sent for broadcast as a 'preview' on *The Ed Sullivan Show*.

For *It's Trad, Dad!* Lester's two young protagonists (Craig Douglas and Helen Shapiro) rush around a TV studio complex, encountering a range of trad jazz bands, and he shot three numbers a day. The pressure meant Lester 'reverted to television techniques', filming with multiple cameras to maximise the editing options in one take: 'The basis of the technique I've used ever since was forged in those two and a half weeks of shooting.'[78]

On their hunt for bands and DJs, Lester showed the couple being chased in and out of different programmes by a uniformed commissionaire, and guests on a political discussion show physically hitting each other. He refused to bore people, he explained of his approach. Most significantly, the film built to a big documentary-style final dance sequence, with exuberant multi-camera energy capturing the crowd's tangible enjoyment – a clear dry run for the increasingly frenzied finale to the concert in *AHDN*.

Lester also wasn't afraid to mock the attitude of directors, who were usually much older than the artists they were tasked with capturing. In *It's Trad Dad!* we see one director listening to the cricket commentary rather than the band he's recording.

But there are plenty of moments of un-ironic appreciation for TV too. We can sense Lester's joy at directing the Beatles in the inclusion during the rehearsal of 'If I Fell' of the viewfinder shots – making the audience aware of the medium putting across the message. And, during the concert, we watch Spinetti humming along in quiet contentment as the multi-headed beast of the Beatles is captured in multiple monitors.

The glowing presentation of 'And I Love Her' is a sincere TV moment. The edit lingers on the boys refracted through the wall of monitors in the gallery, then pans up to reveal them in the studio – still reproduced in camera monitors – and finally mixes to the

Through the viewfinder with the Beatles

full-screen image. The effect is a celebration of the multiplied impact of the four and the medium's role in transmitting their charisma.

The Beatles themselves had emerged as naturals in this new medium. Apart from the evening broadcasts on Radio Luxembourg, always something of an ordeal for the listener, there was no legal pop music radio to rival the BBC's dominance through the Light Programme, which suffered a union-mandated limit on how much recorded music could be played – the so-called 'needle time' restriction. The Beatles claimed new ground in the cosy arenas of traditional televisual light entertainment such as *Sunday Night at the London Palladium* and *Thank Your Lucky Stars*. Their natural wit and charm worked well on formats featuring an older generation of variety performers, such as Morecambe and Wise.

The scene in the ad agency where George mocks the youth TV presenter Susan Campey suggests that the mushrooming new youth TV formats might be more about older TV executives exploiting young consumers than an authentic celebration of youth culture.

Some contemporary pop TV was banal. On the Beatles' first appearance on an early episode of *Ready, Steady, Go!* (4 October

1963), the questions the show's compere, singer Dusty Springfield, is given to ask were as inane as those hurled at the fictional press conference in *AHDN*: for example, asking John if he had false teeth, 'as they always look so even'. One of Ringo's press conference 'ad-libs' appears to have its origins in the band's live appearance on the show on 20 March 1964, when Cathy McGowan asked him, 'Do you think you're a mod? Do you know what a mod is, Ringo?' To which he replied, 'No, I'm not a mod, or a rocker. I'm a mocker.'

More often, the band mimed their songs in such pop show appearances. While filmed that way, the fictional premise of the band's performances in *AHDN* is that they are playing live. And there's a real-life vindication for the achievement of Lester's fictional alterego – Spinetti's harassed director – in the two-page letter written by BBC TV director Barney Colehan to the boss of BBC Television, explaining the disastrous as-live recording of the band at Liverpool's Empire Theatre on 7 December 1963, and transmitted later the same day. At key moments, the footage often focused on the wrong band member and the sound was frequently inaudible. Colehan wrote in self-exculpatory mitigation:

When the actual recording started it was obvious from the wild behaviour and frantic screaming of the fans, that this sadly under-rehearsed programme would not go according to plan ... The noise in the theatre was so deafening that the Beatles could not hear their own internal balance, and were therefore singing out of tune for some of the time. The camera crew could not hear my instructions due to the ear-splitting noise ... and the pre-arranged shots were useless. I had to resort to bellowing down my microphone in order to convey any instructions whatsoever.[79]

Viewing *AHDN*'s climactic concert in the light of this knowledge only adds to the achievement of this sequence.

It also becomes yet another Lester pop music visual template, this time for the live concert film. There's a Hitchcockian glimpse of the director himself during the first song, 'Tell Me Why', shot from

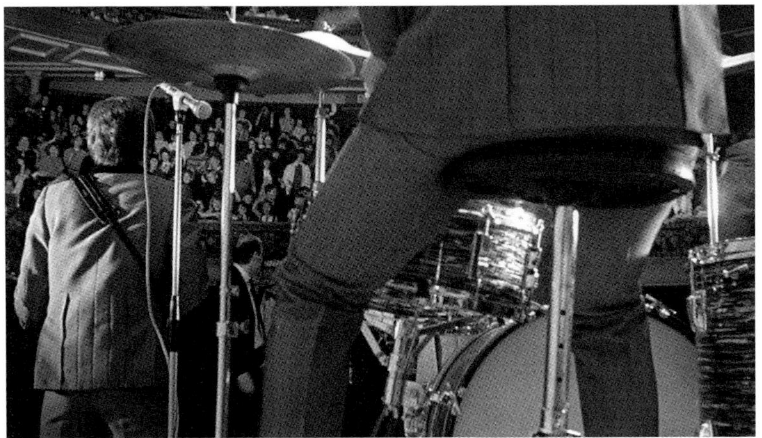

Richard Lester's cameo in *AHDN*, surveying his work during 'Tell Me Why'

behind Ringo, walking from left to right at the front of the stalls, past the stage, stopping to look at the band and taking a moment, smiling, to enjoy the spectacle. There is that marvellous sense of a director who knows he is in sync with the viewer; and capturing the Beatles as if on the small screen, for posterity on the big screen.

4 Women in *A Hard Day's Night*

They've gone potty out there. The whole place is surging with girls.

Norm in AHDN

Please sir, can I have one to surge with, sir?

John

In 1964 screaming girls was the image the general adult population associated with Beatlemania – the very word implying the gendered Victorian medical coinage 'hysteria' (from the Greek for womb). *AHDN* starts with them in the chase through the railway station, but the film's female characters range much more widely and deserve a closer look.

Think back to the schoolgirls on the train, watching the band perform 'I Should Have Known Better'. Once the train has pulled into London and the band are preparing to exit, Pattie Boyd stands by the door looking gormless – fingers in mouth like a toddler.

The infantilised 'dollybird' female is a cliché of 1950s and 60s British screen; it was partly reinforced by advertising – and Boyd, the Smith's Crisps girl in print and Lester's TV commercial, was a model used to offering the expressions required. It's a rare example of a sexist stereotype in the film.

Mostly, women are seen through a comic lens as characters. Anna Quayle's theatrical figure is the standout, but others are more simplistic cartoon-like figures. Two even share the same squeaky post-synced voice: 'Oh, how?' asks the make-up girl as John tells her 'I can get you on the stage', while the woman Ringo tries to chat up after he emerges from the second-hand shop utters a more street-smart, but identically high pitched, 'get out of it, shorty.'

The most dated role is given to Margaret Nolan, future *Carry On* performer, and two months later to be immortalised in the opening title sequence to *Goldfinger* – with scenes from the film projected onto her gold-painted, leather bikini-clad body. In *AHDN* she plays the comedy dumb blonde, a kind of sweet but mute accomplice to Brambell's gallivanting Grandfather, who heads off in borrowed tails to Le Cercle club with Ringo's invitation. By the standards of Benny Hill, it's very mild, and I have always had great

affection for Nolan's sweet-natured presence in films, despite her being the butt of jokes about the size of her chest. Grandfather looks at her low-cut dress and jokes 'I bet you're a great swimmer', and she waves dumbly as he's dragged off at the end. Alun Owen's original script offered her three lines – the first of which was 'You had a lovely little pair, y'see' – all of which were deleted.

It's interesting that scenes with Margaret Nolan, parodying the opening casino sequence in *Dr. No* (1962) that featured Eunice Gayson's sultry and very verbal Sylvia Trench, are intercut with the Beatles in a nightclub, as if to emphasise the contrast between the stuffy and ludicrous world of the old Establishment and the more equal new world of modern Britain. In the nightclub scene we watch as if we were there, but we cannot hear their conversations with the women they meet. While George and Ringo hit the dance floor, John and Paul seem engaged in real chat with sophisticated, possibly posh young women drinking wine; one (future fashion designer Edina Ronay) appears to be with her own boyfriend, her booted leg perched on the table, erotically cradled in his hand.

If *AHDN* captures on film the peak of the band's teen girl appeal, it also documents, for example in the nightclub sequence,

something more complex that was beginning to be reflected in the increasingly mature themes of their songwriting. On *Rubber Soul*, the Beatles' second 1965 album, in songs such as 'Norwegian Wood' and 'You Won't See Me', they encounter independent career women who might not be at the beck and call of their boyfriends. Beyond the nightclub scenes, four such women make brief appearances in *AHDN*.

First, there is the production assistant to Victor Spinetti in the TV gallery, calmly watching proceedings while he despairs, managing timings and giving him a massage after he collapses in relief once the concert is over. As with the secretary in the ad agency later, a truth is revealed about the dual position of women in such occupations: simultaneously of low *official* status, yet evidently trusted for their knowledge and ability, and core to the success of their workplace and their male employer. One could imagine Spinetti's assistant as a Verity Lambert-like talent, waiting for her own big break. Lambert was famously the launch producer of *Doctor Who* in 1963.

During the run-through of 'And I Love Her', watching in the gallery alongside the female PA is the head of make-up. When the performance is over, the director consults the two women together for

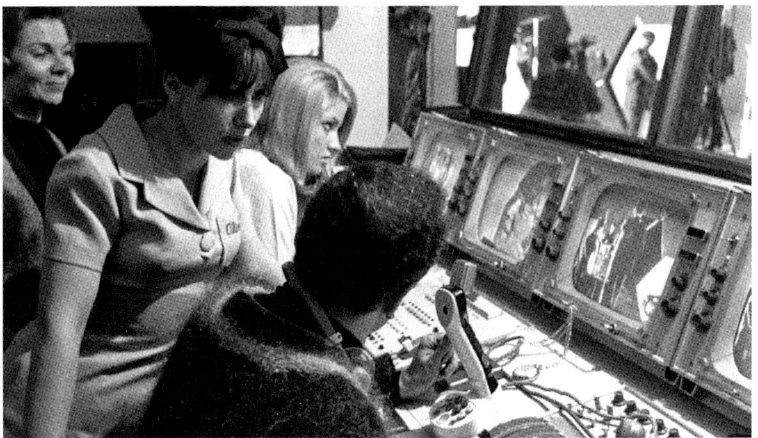

Director consulting the head of make-up – one of several career women in *AHDN*

their notes with a minimal need for words. 'Make-up?' he asks, trusting her professional assessment. 'No, not really,' the head of make-up observes, concisely. 'We'll just powder them off a little for the shine.' Her judgement cements the sense of the Beatles' natural televisual ability.

I particularly like the realism of the film's depiction of these TV craft relationships, accurately reflecting what make-up artists who joined the BBC's make-up school in the mid-1960s have told me – of a generation of young female school-leavers building careers in an important and rapidly expanding female-led industry craft. These women were often very aware of being on the front line of cultural change, as they powdered off old and new generations of entertainers coming through their make-up rooms, just like in the film, in the new screen factories such as BBC Television Centre, which had opened in 1960.

Later, however, we see the head of make-up quite fiercely and physically dragging her make-up artists off set when she finds them lingering unprofessionally by the band as they play 'I'm Happy Just to Dance with You'. I've never found this moment convincing, but assume Lester wanted to create a sense of these slightly older women as equally bewitched by the spell of the Beatles.

The third female character of special interest is Millie,
the woman John briefly encounters in the backstage corridors,
immediately after the Beatles' 'Can't Buy Me Love' frolics in the field.

Comic actress Anna Quayle is the scene stealer of the entire
film. 'Hello,' she declares warmly, catching John's eye so he stops,
while his bandmates pass on by. But she cannot place him. 'Oh, wait
a minute, don't tell me, you're …' John denies any resemblance to the
unknown celebrity.

This chance encounter in the corridor is full of mystery, partly
doubled in a wall mirror as yet another play on identity, and has the
surreal mood of similar scenes in *A Show Called Fred*. Who is Millie,
this older theatrical figure? Actress? Producer? Designer? Director?
With her mohair jumper, glasses on a chain that she fidgets with, like
Spinetti with his stopwatch, she offers a subtle visual echo of his fussy
artistic persona. As if riffing on the eighteenth-century costumes in
the background to the film, the scene is a battle of equal wits, like a
flirty mini-Sheridan play, in which she fails to quite place John, and
he plays along. I like to imagine a different screenplay that might
have given more screen time to this kind of female character over the
Brambell plotline. Quayle had recently won a Tony as Best Featured

Actress in the musical *Stop the World – I Want to Get Off*. *AHDN* was her first film role and she remembered completing the scene in only two takes, thanks, she said, to John's fearlessness.[80]

The fourth career woman and one of the most intriguing in *AHDN* is the Julie Christie-like gatekeeper at the ad agency, which George accidentally wanders into while searching for the canteen. The nameless 'Secretary' is played by Alison Seebohm, who was in real life nearly four years older than George. Described in the script as 'a smart young woman typing busily', we see someone much more complex. Superficially a secretary, she is seated behind a typewriter, but she defies every stereotype of the traditional office assistant. Shoes off on the desk, cigarette in hand, she smiles, coolly appraises George for his potential, embarrassing him into lowering his gaze. It is an exact gender-reversed enactment of Grandfather's later challenge to Ringo to 'embarrass a Sheila with your cool appraising stare'.

'Holding the gaze' is something I remember being taught on an NLP (neuro-linguistic programming) career course for female confidence I was sent on as a TV news anchor forty years after the making of *AHDN*. NLP emerged in the 1970s out of psychological theories of behaviour, to become a popular career coaching tool in the corporate world. To see it deployed here has real power. The fact that looking down in embarrassment offers an opportunity for George to check out her legs only emphasises the sense of confidence she exudes. There is electricity in the air; a flirtation of equals. As a sophisticated London woman, she might well have the advantage. She picks up the phone to report her find, smiling at George while she talks about him, and it's made clear that her boss trusts her judgement: 'Well,' she says after a pause, 'I think *you* ought to see him.'

When she leads George into her boss's office, she's mostly silent, but Kenneth Haigh's ad executive Simon refers to her without needing to make eye contact, a sure sign of how closely they understand and communicate with each other. Even when it appears she's brought in a faulty product, he's not cross with her:

'Hello? I've got one'

SIMON   Oh my god, he's a natural.
SECRETARY (anxiously) Well I did tell them not to send us any more real ones.
SIMON   They ought to know by now the phonies are much easier
               to handle. Still, he's a good type.

Perched on Simon's desk throughout the encounter, she appears more an equal to bounce ideas off than the hapless, silent Adrian, following orders and too scared to voice his awareness that George might be someone more important than his boss realises.

Another woman in this scene, if only on a photo placard, is, in Simon's words, 'Only Susan Campey, our resident teenager. You'll have to love her. She's your symbol.' Even allowing for the fictional nature of this scene, it's not hard to see a mockery of female youth TV presenters such as Cathy McGowan of *Ready, Steady Go!*, implying they were empty-headed constructs of big business. Even if it's not her sex that's the intended target, George's put-down seems tinged with Alun Owen's at best accidental sexism: 'Oh, you mean that posh bird who gets everything wrong? She's a drag. A well-known drag. We turn the sound down on her and say rude things.'

In *AHDN*, the women journalists we encounter in the press conference scene are in their own way as un-clued up as the arrogant bouffant-haired man who asks repeatedly about the band's haircuts, and their attitude is just as ripe for mockery. One is rather serious and asks with pointed gravitas: 'Do you have any hobbies?', while the other, older, woman, with strong Vidal Sassoon-style bob and cat's-eye black eyeliner, flirts with Ringo, while asking increasingly inane questions about what he calls his collar.

At the press conference, there is a duo of much older women in formal hats and suits, the posh version of the kind of Dandy Nichols-housewife in the street who would become a regular feature of Lester's films, notably *Help!* The women smile charmingly at Ringo, while wolfing down the sandwiches the boys never get. I've always been intrigued by these two women. Were they from the Women's Institute in-house magazine? Did they even care who the Beatles were? Or were they just there for the sandwiches?

In fact, female journalists such as Maureen Cleave and photographer Fiona Adams were vitally important in grasping early on the Beatles' talent and importance, and conveying their charm to both a youth and an older mainstream audience. Cleave even helped improve the lyrics of the film's title song. Paul McCartney remembered Cleave with fondness when I interviewed him in 2021.

There is a missing woman from *AHDN* worth considering. In Owen's original script each of the Beatles had a solo scene: John with Millie, George in the ad agency, Ringo with the Boy all survive. Paul's solo adventure should have followed Ringo's eviction from the Turk's Head pub but was deleted from the final edit.

Paul's adventure starts in similar fashion to George's, as he stumbles into a TV rehearsal room and encounters a 'very young and lovely' actress (Isla Blair) in period costume engrossed in rehearsing her lines. The script directions state, 'She is acting in the manner of an eighteenth-century coquette.' Paul offers her advice about how to play it more naturally. It's a more serious and semi-romantic interlude than any of the other scenes.

Paul had studied English Literature for A-level – we saw how he quoted poetry at the opera girl extras – and he was a regular theatregoer by this time. His allegedly awkward acting is often cited to explain why the episode was dropped, and Lester has suggested Paul overthought the scene, given his much greater knowledge of and exposure to professional stagecraft through his then girlfriend, actress Jane Asher.

However, even on paper, Owen's rather portentous scripted dialogue looks challenging and borderline misogynistic. It refers to 'scrubbers' and features a long anecdote about Paul making treacle toffee with his mum, and though Lester replaced some of those lines on the shoot with something lighter, there is an uncomfortably dated air to the discussion about women's personae. It was complex to shoot, filmed over two days, with the camera sometimes circling Paul and Blair as they played the scene. It also would have broken the rule Lester and Epstein had agreed on to have no love interest.

Perhaps the scene needed the presence of another breakthrough northern star of the new generation such as Rita Tushingham to match Paul and make the encounter more relaxed. Lester took the attempted arch and sexually playful mood of this deleted scene and turned it into an entire film in his next project, *The Knack ... and How to Get It* (1965), starring Tushingham.

What about the other women, in small roles, who we *do* see in *AHDN*?

Barmaids offer both the promise of refreshment and stern rebuke: at the theatre press conference, the elegant older blonde woman in a black sweater, proffering trays of sandwiches with a smile; the young dark-haired barmaid pouring Paul an ale he never gets to drink; and, of course, later, on Ringo's parading adventures, the sour-faced landlady of the Turk's Head, a magnificent symbol of British culture, who insists her hard, curled-at-the-edges sandwich 'was fresh this morning. 2/9'. She sends Ringo on his way after his inept dart throwing hits her parrot's cage.

Former Miss World Rosemarie Frankland as one of the showgirls (photograph by Bert Cann)

Throughout their time at the TV theatre, the Beatles constantly encounter professional working female dancers. There are the Lionel Blair dancers in sequinned leotards and ostrich-plumed headpieces improvising a dance to a jolly piano version of 'I'm Happy Just to Dance with You'. There's a cohort of chorus-line dancers, with their distinctive black-and-white bobbled caps and costumes sitting in the circle – 'Look, it's a bird,' quips John, flicking the feathers on one of their hats as he walks by; they grin and take it in their stride. When going up a narrow spiral staircase, John mimes being a dirty old man. It's evidence of how knowing the film is, and how – except in the casino scene – it does not deliberately mock or denigrate women.

In a film peppered with figures from popular culture, there is tall, elegant Rosemarie Frankland. Featuring in a small scene where George, Paul and John are discussing the disappearance of Ringo, she has no lines but does look slightly perturbed as George fiddles with her skimpy shoulder strap, like a schoolboy with the fastening on a school satchel. The scene works much better with the knowledge that she would have been a familiar face at the time. Perhaps it's most useful to compare it to brief celebrity cameos by the likes of David Dimbleby and Cilla Black in TV comedy shows such as *The Goodies* (1970–82), or Johnny Depp making a guest appearance on a farewell special episode of *The Fast Show* (26 December 2000). Frankland's appearance reinforces what Lester so powerfully wanted to convey – that the Beatles were turning the world of popular culture and entertainment upside down, and everyone wanted to be in their orbit.

Examining the presence of women in *AHDN* reveals how the film, while always making clear that the Beatles are lively young heterosexual men, never relies – in their encounters with females – on promoting the kind of stereotype that has dated so many British social realist films of its time. Compare it with *Billy Liar*. Released seven months before shooting began on *AHDN*, its director John Schlesinger used a similar pop art style, combining advertising, surreal fantasy and documentary naturalism. Tom Courtenay's hero is a northern dreamer, not dissimilar to the Beatles. But the plot, based on the play by Keith Waterhouse and Ted Willis, relies on three crude stereotypes of women, focused as it is on Billy's desire to get laid. There is Rita the slutty one, Barbara the frigid one and Liz the free spirit, who hopes he won't mind that she's not a virgin.

There is one small sadness of truth versus fantasy in *AHDN*, though: John was married to Cynthia, whom he'd met as an equal – a fellow student at the Liverpool School of Art. Their son Julian was eleven months old when shooting began on the film. Like many couples at the time, they married when she fell pregnant, five years before the law was amended to allow the NHS to prescribe the contraceptive pill to unmarried women and partially decriminalised abortion. Unplanned pregnancy was the plot of many a male-focused kitchen sink drama at the time, from *Saturday Night and Sunday Morning* (1960) to *A Kind of Loving* (1962). *A Taste of Honey*, based on Shelagh Delaney's 1958 play, was a rare example of a female point of view on the subject. Part of the fiction of *AHDN* was the illusion of the Beatles' 'availability' to fans. So Cynthia and her fascinating perspective as one of the few young women at the heart of Beatlemania was ignored. After *AHDN*'s release, it would not be until Waris Hussein's *A Touch of Love* (1969), based on Margaret Drabble's 1965 novel *The Millstone*, and also partly shot with schoolgirls at Marylebone station, that we would find a great Swinging London film that offered a wholly female point of view on the accidental pregnancy plot.

I like to think that one day someone might make a Lester-style film about the escapades of the Beatles' first wives and fiancées, Cynthia, Maureen, Jane and Pattie. Cynthia and Pattie were smuggled out of one hotel in laundry baskets,[81] and the women supported each other like members of a secret wartime operations unit.

5 Reception and What They Did Next

They're 'fab' and all the other pimply hyperboles.

Simon, the advertising executive in *AHDN*

Between the contract agreement in October 1963 and the film's release in July 1964, the Beatles had become a global phenomenon. Seventy-three million Americans had watched them perform on *The Ed Sullivan Show* on their first US visit in February 1964, and they had performed in Denmark, Hong Kong and toured Australia, with more than 300,000 people turning out in Adelaide to line their route from the airport. The *AHDN* soundtrack album spent fourteen weeks at number one on the American Billboard charts.

As Walter Shenson recalled in 1998:

The people from United Artists in New York, who had really left me alone completely up to that point, called me on the Monday after the Sunday the Beatles were on *The Ed Sullivan Show*. They were so excited. They said, 'Do you need any more money? What can we do to get you going?' And I replied, 'Everything's on schedule, don't worry about it. We're right into it; we'll give you a good picture.' And we did.[82]

The first screening took place after a Hollywood dinner at a United Artists executive's home, in the presence of Billy Wilder. Executive producer Dave Picker recalls how, after it ended, there was

utter silence. No one knew what to say ... It was such an anti-Hollywood type movie ... It stunned them ... It breaks every rule that even the best of the Hollywood movies followed. Nobody disliked it, but nobody had expected what they saw.

Eventually, one studio executive, Bob Benjamin, turned around to Picker and said, 'I don't know what that was about, but I think we're going to make a lot of money.'[83]

The film's 'Royal World Premiere' on 6 July 1964 at the London Pavilion was a huge success. Screaming crowds, restrained by struggling police officers, filled Piccadilly Circus, which had seen nothing like it since VE Day in 1945. As the curtains opened, the big opening shot Lester had so carefully constructed with that crashing chord and a fade-up from black was ruined, as the cinema organist continued to play his medley of Beatles hits over the first seconds of the film: 'I had made sure that there were no credits or titles before the first chord that opens *A Hard Day's Night*. But this mighty Wurlitzer was still finishing off his version of "Can't Buy Me Love" and ran over it.'[84]

Afterwards, at the reception at the Dorchester Hotel, Princess Margaret, clearly enamoured of the Beatles, lingered much longer

The Beatles at the London Pavilion premiere, 6 July 1964 (photograph by Bert Cann)

than expected. A hungry George Harrison, told by Shenson that they couldn't go to dinner until the royal party left, went up to HRH and told her, 'Ma'am, Walter says we can't eat until you leave, and we're hungry.'[85]

The Liverpool premiere was four days later at the city's Odeon cinema. The band were nervous about how they, rather than the film, would be received. 'Big shots? Who did they think they were?' John recalled in 1967.

We couldn't say it, but we really didn't like going back to Liverpool. Being local heroes made us nervous ... We felt embarrassed in our suits and being very clean. We were worried that friends might think we'd sold out – which we had, in a way.[86]

In the end, 200,000 people turned out on the streets for their civic reception at the Town Hall and balcony appearance, where John, with his characteristic mischievous nature, gave a Hitler salute. The Granada newsreel footage captures Ringo immediately telling him, 'don't'. Their reception was confirmation that the boys had done good and made their hometown proud.

Press reviews were almost unanimously favourable, and many reviewers, of an older generation, admitted their own sense of surprise at this attractive combination of anarchy and animal energy. Cecil Wilson in the *Daily Mail* compared these 'four adenoidal young anarchists from Liverpool' to the Marx Brothers[87]. So did the *Sunday Times*' Dilys Powell, who admitted she had been dreading the film. Instead, she was delighted to find

a sharply professional piece, directed with great dash ... boldly photographed ... and smartly edited and acted as well as thrummed and bawled with the most likeable aplomb by the Sacred Four. Deafening of course. But it really is restoring to find in the British cinema, apt to waver between devoted amateurism and mad polish, the seeming spontaneity of this exercise in anarchy.[88]

Another reviewer, Isabel Quigley, appreciated the way the film showed the cage of their fame 'from all angles' and 'without sentimentality'. 'Their whole style', she concluded, 'makes Cliff Richard last week seem like a cream-fed domestic cat compared with a litter of perfectly groomed jaguars.'[89] Arthur Knight, writing in the US weekly magazine *Saturday Review* and taken with its *nouvelle vague* energy, reached for his own animal metaphor, describing them in the 'Can't Buy Me Love' breakout sequence 'as fresh and untrammelled as the frisking of young colts'.[90]

Many reviewers picked out the Beatles' natural on-screen charm and charisma. Felix Barker in the *London Evening News* praised their 'immense off-beat charm' and the film's 'terrific gusto. And something else besides. A really unexpected quality. Sophistication.'[91] Leonard Mosley in the *Daily Express* described the film as 'palpitating cinema' and admits, 'For the first time I understand why Ringo has such a following of fans.'[92]

Michael Thornton in the *Sunday Express* also had an epiphany: 'I would never have believed before I saw it, the extent to which the four boys emerge as personalities in their own right.' He was one of a number to be convinced by the script's capture of 'the strange elusive idiom of the Merseybeat'. He also detected a 'glimmer of pathos' in the Beatles' celebrity entrapment, 'imprisoned in the gigantic goldfish bowl of their own success'.[93]

The *News of the World* called it 'an all-action all-screaming assault on the eyes and ears',[94] which manages to be both insult and praise. Not all saw the film as original, though. Patrick Gibbs in the *Daily Telegraph* thought the script offered 'essentially one of those backstage pieces so familiar in musical films',[95] but was perhaps astute in observing that Wilfrid Brambell 'becomes tiresome both in the writing and the playing'. He did, however, single out the comic talent of the Beatles as a team: 'engagingly provocative and wonderfully photogenic'.

The *Times* film critic complained about the film's style, objecting to the excessively New Wave editing and 'obtrusively handheld' camerawork.[96] The *Financial Times* reviewer, perhaps channelling Richard Vernon's bowler-hatted gent in the first-class carriage, complained of the 'shapeless improvisation' and 'pictures and dialogue that are hard to see and hear', finding the 'inconsequence and indiscipline and artificial striving for speed ... tiring and tedious'. 'Informality is fashionable,' he sneered, 'but it has no merit in itself.'[97]

The cineaste *Monthly Film Bulletin* (now part of the BFI's *Sight and Sound* magazine) was sniffy about the film's 'neo-nouvelle vague air'[98] and complained of too much screaming. Anne Scott James in her *Daily Mail* column, also on the side of Richard Vernon, one suspects, thought there was a cruelty about some of the Beatles' encounters, 'without one twinge of pity for human beings, particularly the old'.[99]

The film was released in the US six weeks later, on 12 August. In its most famous US review, Andrew Sarris of the *Village Voice* called it 'the Citizen Kane of jukebox musicals',[100] while *Time* magazine in a review headlined 'Yeah? Yeah. Yeah!'[101] described *AHDN* as 'one of the smoothest, freshest, funniest films ever made solely for purposes of exploitation. It seems better than it ought to be simply because the Beatles prove themselves disarming personalities.' However, it found the humour sometimes forced and 'the North country slang impenetrable'.

United Artists had built up much hype around the film, including by inviting the members of two Beatles fan clubs from New York to camp overnight at the cinema where it was premiering. Debbie Gendler, the New Jersey Fan Club president, said they were promised hot chocolate and doughnuts to pass the night, with guarantees that they would get tickets.[102]

Like many fans, Debbie went to see the film multiple times. Larger than life on the big screen, *AHDN* offered fans what they'd been waiting for: 'I got a chance to really see them close up.'[103] In the long summer 'silly season', short on regular politics, British newspapers could generate copy. The *Sunday Express* ('Hard Day's

Night for a Girl of Seven')[104] reported on Nottingham children spending all day in the cinema, and mothers going searching for their lost offspring at the local picture house.

The film had made close to a 200 per cent profit pre-opening, on the strength of the album sales.[105] And there was huge demand for prints of the film, with United Artists announcing a planned saturation release during post-production. In all, 1,000 prints were requested in the US, 110 made for the UK and between 1,500 and 1,800 for the rest of the world.[106] *AHDN* was nominated for two Academy Awards, for Best Screenplay and Best Original Score for George Martin's jazzy arrangements.

The film was successful abroad, with a variety of titles. Italy's *Tutti per uno* (All for One) was apt and unknowingly anticipated Lester's future *Musketeers* films. But the French title – *Quatre garçons dans le vent* (Four Boys in the Wind) – most satisfyingly captured the *nouvelle vague* feel of *AHDN*. West Germany's *Yeah! Yeah! Yeah!* was closest to the 'Beatlemania' working title in tone, but its German dialogue was wildly different from the original, attempting its own culturally coherent surreal take. Hence references to such specifics as a Hamlet soliloquy and mods and rockers are replaced by riffs on Fidel Castro, Günter Grass's novel *The Tin Drum* and quotes from German poetry. In the press conference scene, Paul talks intensely about German cinema and wanting to make a film called *The Scream* with Ingmar Bergman, while in the bathroom sequence, John's ad-libs are almost entirely un-World War II related.[107]

In Portugal, then under dictatorship, the film wasn't released until February 1965 and classified for adults only. Western pop music was, of course, also seen as a subversive threat to youth by Communist regimes in Eastern Europe, so it made headlines in the US when Radio Free Europe reporters got special access to interview the band on the train during the first day of shooting, for a programme to be broadcast into Poland.[108]

The relentless pace of the Beatles' life continued, and Lester's output also increased, thanks to the acclaim that came his way, with another two films produced and released within a year. *The Knack … and How to Get It* – also in black and white and loosely inspired by the Ann Jellicoe play – was awarded the Palme d'Or at the Cannes Film Festival, the only major film prize Lester has won and sweet recognition from the home of the *nouvelle vague*. The film has a surreal quality, with housemates clambering over furniture blocking up the stairs, and the documentary-style real reactions of ordinary people watching Rita Tushingham on a bed, being pulled around the streets of London, has the freshness of early factual TV entertainment shows. It's been suggested that Lester portrayed these young people playing against a Greek chorus of disapproval, and it was much imitated. The airy content of *The Knack … and How to Get It*, including an extended comic riff on rape and jokes about a long line of interchangeable empty-faced dollybirds queuing up for a session with the womanising Tolen (Ray Brooks), has not aged well, unlike the elegant jazz soundtrack by John Barry, which is thrilling. Above all, for all its comedy, it lacks the warmth of *AHDN*.

By the time Lester and the Beatles reunited for *Help!* the band were smoking a lot of pot. Ringo recalled: 'Dick Lester knew that very little would get done after lunch. In the afternoon we very seldom got past the first line of the script'; while George acknowledged: 'we pushed Dick Lester to the limit of his patience. And he was very, very easy going.'[109]

The film had a silly cartoon-like plot about Ringo being pursued by an Indian cult for human sacrifice. Lester conceived it as Wilkie Collins's *The Moonstone* as photographed by Jasper Johns, but it also smacked of too many James Bond films. Like a high-budget version of a Spike Milligan TV show, it was full of deconstructed reality, riffs on the British Establishment and imperial self-image, and Lester's comedy repertory stalwarts, including Leo McKern, Victor Spinetti and Roy Kinnear, plus the high-class cool of Establishment club alumna Eleanor Bron. Shot in colour, there were radiantly glamorous locations in the Austrian Alps and the Bahamas.

Children who saw *Help!* on TV years after the Beatles split probably loved it more than *AHDN*. At least when they were little. As John remembered in 1980:

The movie was out of our control. With *AHDN* we had a lot of input and it was semi-realistic. But with *Help!*, Dick Lester didn't tell us what it was about. I realise, looking back, how advanced it was. It was a precursor for the Batman Pow! Wow! on TV – that kind of stuff. But he never explained it to us … partly because we were smoking marijuana for breakfast during that period. Nobody could communicate with us; it was all glazed eyes and giggling all the time. In our own world.[110]

The resulting film, while still entertaining, notably for Lester's further development of pop video treatments of songs, feels more of a construct – making the band appear, in John's phrase, like extras in their own feature.

The playwright Joe Orton was commissioned to take an existing film outline and write a full script for a third Beatles feature, *Up Against It* – but his script was, even for the 1960s, wildly sexist, and considered too transgressive in its sexual themes (Joe Orton transgressive? Surely not). Still, Lester pursued the idea of a version starring Mick Jagger and Ian McKellen. But it was not to be. Orton was found murdered on 9 August 1967, the day he was due to go to Twickenham Studios to discuss the film. A version of this revised screenplay has since been made into a BBC Radio 4 drama.

Lester's career divided into pre- and post-*The Bed Sitting Room* (1969) – a film about a world powered entirely by delusion. The failure of this surreal post-apocalyptic satire saw him turn to carefully recreated period and action dramas: notably, *The Three Musketeers* (1973) and its sequels, which featured a fab four from literature. But all of them, together with *Royal Flash* (1975) and *Robin and Marian* (1976) and his two Superman films,[111] subverted ideas of heroes and glory, with Lester's trademark slapstick touches.

What about the Beatles themselves? The relentless pace of their lives speeded up even more as they flew across the globe to perform. The bizarre press conferences, as mocked in *AHDN*, continued, and became more surreal, as the band found the press turning up everywhere with their inane questions, even at the hospital where Ringo went to have his tonsils out.

Despite some discomfort at seeing themselves on screen, they all agreed they'd like to make more films. Paul McCartney felt most misrepresented by his persona in *AHDN*: 'I was typecast as the cute one. It was strange being reduced to a couple of shorthand characteristics in the eyes of the world.'[112] It must have been particularly tough as he was always the most cultural savvy of the Beatles. And he noticed all the factual details in representations. In *The Beatles Anthology* (1995) he pointed out his annoyance that the 1994 biopic *Backbeat* showed the John character singing the Little Richard song 'Long Tall Sally', when it was always Paul's signature number. 'I was not amused.'[113] And George observed:

The Dick Lester version of our lives in *[A] Hard Day's Night* and *Help!* made it look fun and games: a good romp? That was fair in the films but in the real world there was never any doubt. The Beatles were doomed. Your own space, man, it's so important. That's why we were doomed because we didn't have any. It's like monkeys in a zoo. They die.[114]

Still, seeds of their future artistry emerged amidst the silliness. George had his first encounter with the sitar during the shoot of *Help!*, going up to talk to the group of real Indian musicians playing versions of Beatles' hits in the restaurant scene.

Magical Mystery Tour (1967), which they made by themselves, was a critical and audience disaster, proving that the Beatles needed a ringmaster like Lester to make the best of their larking around. Watching them pretend to be wizards is, for me, that unimaginable thing – embarrassing. But the colour film, with its bold improvised approach, has developed a certain arthouse charm in the decades since its disastrous black-and-white premiere on BBC1 on Christmas Day in 1967. The dream sequence, where John piles endless spaghetti on the plate of distressed Aunt Jessie, feels worthy of Buñuel.

Beyond their rich offering of original songs, the Beatles had little to do with the animated feature *Yellow Submarine* (1968), other than a brief live-action coda appearance. But the film's original psychedelic themes and style somehow captured them and the era, and have made it an enduring classic. It's what *Help!* perhaps tried to be: a genuine fantasy adventure with the cultural phenomenon of the Beatles at its heart.

In recent years, much attention has been given to the new documentary possibilities afforded by cleaning up original footage – from Ron Howard's *Eight Days a Week – The Touring Years* (2016) to the widely acclaimed reworking of Michael Lindsay-Hogg's *Let It Be* (1970), successfully rebirthed by Peter Jackson as *The Beatles: Get Back* (2021) for Disney+. Perhaps what's been forgotten is the Beatles' own TV documentary follow-up to *AHDN – The Beatles at Shea Stadium* (1966), which captured the opening night of their major US tour on 15 August 1965.

The concert broke the world record for the largest rock concert audience and box-office take to date. Like *AHDN*, it used multiple cameras – twelve for the concert sequence – featured the fans as well as backstage footage and voiceover interviews, and gave a convincing sense of the even greater hysteria that had grown around the band. The strange disproportion of their lives was captured in multiple ways: in the distance they must run to their tiny stage in the centre of a baseball field, the number of warm-up acts for their own short thirty-minute act and the inadequacy of the audio system for projecting their performance above the screams. The band and their artistry are lost within the vortex. Filmed a year after *AHDN*, it shows why their concert touring had become a hell from which they had to escape.

The solo film careers of all four men have their roots in *AHDN*. Ringo, the natural, won acclaim in the film of Terry Southern's

The Magic Christian (1969), with old Lester accomplice Peter Sellers, and *That'll Be the Day* (1973), going on to meet his second wife, Bond girl Barbara Bach, on the set of *Caveman* (1981), and settling in Monte Carlo and ultimately California.

Paul McCartney's ambition saw him take up the offer to write music for the British social realist comedy drama *The Family Way* (1966) and later the title song for the hugely successful Bond film *Live and Let Die* (1973). But his desire to make a film musical resulted in the curious folly of *Give My Regards to Broad Street* (1984), which he both wrote and starred in. With its strange combination of acting talent (Ralph Richardson, Tracey Ullman), London landmarks, such as BBC Broadcasting House and the eponymous railway station near Liverpool Street, nostalgic culture clash (the Teds versus ballroom dancers sequence), plus Ringo in a boat in a strange outfit, it seemed to bear ghostly traces of *AHDN*.

It was John, with his unfiltered fast mouth, who showed the most promise and won critical praise as a screen actor. He had a small but key role in Lester's anti-war satire *How I Won the War*. And Lester cites John as one of the most influential people in his life, alongside Buster Keaton and Spike Milligan.[115] However, he was soon sidetracked into the often-mocked conceptual art projects of his partnership with Yoko Ono.

But it was George, captured in *AHDN* as the sceptic, the laconic rebel, who made the greatest impact. He was a fan of *Monty Python's Flying Circus* (1969–74) from the start, who drew directly on the surreal comedy of Milligan and Lester, and found liberation from his own band history, appearing in a cameo in the Eric Idle mockumentary *The Rutles: All You Need Is Cash* (1978). George became a key figure in independent British cinema, remortgaging his home to bail out *Monty Python's Life of Brian* (1979) when EMI withdrew its funding, and helped the Monty Python team face down the controversy generated by a Christian political campaign against the film. He set up HandMade Films, which was to end in financial chaos, and cause George great torment. But in its heyday, with him at the helm, it produced such quirky landmarks of British cinema as *The Long Good Friday* (1980), *Time Bandits* (1981), *Mona Lisa* (1986) and *Withnail and I* (1987). The films he backed were a striking contrast to the period lavishness of Merchant Ivory films, which at the time garnered most acclaim and industry awards. Cocking a snook, you might say.

What of *AHDN*'s initial post-cinematic life? It had drawn audiences on its regular cinematic screenings throughout the 1960s in the US, where Shenson continued to promote it, while in Britain it attracted a new generation of young fans, who discovered the Beatles through their films on TV, where it was often screened over Christmas. *AHDN* was first screened on UK TV on Monday 28 December 1970, at 4.05 pm on BBC1. John reportedly watched it and was inspired to write 'I'm the Greatest', which eventually appeared on Ringo's eponymous 1973 album.[116]

But it really made its mark when it was programmed as part of a BBC2 Beatles 'season' at Christmas 1979, which screened all four of the band's feature films and TV specials made between 1964 and 1970, including the Shea Stadium documentary. *AHDN* went out on Christmas Day at 3 pm, scheduled directly against the Queen's speech. Broadcast on the alternative cultural BBC TV channel, there was the sense at last of its recognition as an arthouse film – a celluloid landmark that challenged the Establishment.

6 Legacy: An Early Clue to the New Direction

The fundamental premise of *AHDN* – its fictionalised madcap adventure format – spawned dozens of instant imitations on both sides of the Atlantic. Most of them awful. The first Herman's Hermits film, *Hold On!* (1966), was, as lead singer Peter Noone recalled, 'basically a pure copy. Everyone was making one. Four or five guys running round being chased by a lot of girls.'[117] *The Mini-Mob*, influenced also by *Help!*, featured comedy stalwarts such as Roy Kinnear and Irene Handl and a mob of female mods kidnapping supposedly eligible English men – including Georgie Fame. On the plus side, the mob was racially diverse. That's the only plus.

Perhaps most surprising was the deeply inferior *Ferry Cross the Mersey* (1964), released only five months after *AHDN* and produced by Brian Epstein to promote more of his acts. It has the benefit of Gilbert Taylor's beautiful photography and a historically fascinating capture of lost Liverpool locations, including the Cavern Club, but is otherwise atrocious. There's even a plot element set at an art school (referencing Lennon and original Beatle Stuart Sutcliffe's real lives), with Margaret Nolan as the naked life model. Co-written by Tony Warren, the acclaimed creator of the TV drama serial *Coronation Street* (1960–), it doesn't just lack Alun Owen's playful originality, its desperately old-fashioned tone features a song competition plot, racist jokes about the Liverpool Chinese community and a prominent cameo by DJ Jimmy Savile – now known to have been one of Britain's worst paedophiles.[118]

More positively, the other immediate cinematic response to *AHDN* was John Boorman's debut feature, *Catch Us If You Can* (1965), for the Dave Clark Five – which even has a similarly *nouvelle vague* Beatles-esque title. Shot like *AHDN* in exquisite black and white, it takes the idea of advertising pop culture into intriguing territory. Barbara Ferris plays a Susan Campey-like advertising figurehead, seeking the band's help to escape from her role marketing British meat. They run away together, defacing her own image on posters.

The film has an unexpectedly melancholic mood, though its opening title sequence features the band bouncing on a trampoline, unmistakably evocative of the 'Can't Buy Me Love' sequence. All Boorman's grail quest motifs, Bath and Devon locations, talented character actors like Yootha Joyce and fancy dress can't cover for the gaping hole at the heart of the film – the band's lack of charisma. It is one of rock and roll cinema's great what-ifs that Elvis contacted Boorman after seeing it, hoping to take a new direction, but they never did make a film together.[119]

Peter Watkins's *Privilege* (1967) can be viewed as a more pessimistic and political spun-out version of the advertising agency scene in *AHDN*. The film came from an idea by Johnny Speight – the writer Lester originally wanted for his Beatles film – who had watched a rather chilling documentary about the management of the Canadian teen star Paul Anka. Set in the near future, this science-fiction dystopia portrays pop star Steven Shorter, played by the former Manfred Mann lead singer Paul Jones, as a mentally fragile prisoner of the music industry, run by Establishment figures. The scenes of fan hysteria that so troubled the Beatles' political critics and indeed *AHDN*'s DOP, Gilbert Taylor, are just as powerful and given sinister meaning here.

While right-wing and Christian morality campaigners in the US saw Communist-style brainwashing in the fan hysteria, Watkins suggested a ruthless capitalist form of social control. At one point, one of the executives takes Shorter to the office tower to look down on the masses below and lectures him about these 'stunted little creatures, with primitive emotions that are, in themselves, dangerous ... You're our chance, Steven. They identify with you. They love you. You can lead them into a better way of life. A fruitful conformity.'

Privilege is a period curio in many ways, not least for its idea that the Church of England might win back influence through pop stars (even allowing for Christian Cliff Richard's activism), but its warning about a new British nationalism seems increasingly prescient in the light of the growth of UKIP and Reform UK. The genuine fan distress in both *AHDN* and *Privilege* could be interchangeable, but for the colour photography.

Significant parts of *Privilege* play out in the boardroom, with discussions of how changes in youth fashion are timetabled and agreed in advance. In one scene, as the board discuss the agenda item 'the youth of the future', models parade through the meeting in the planned new softer retro Edwardian look, like a nightmare version of George's encounter with the grotty shirts.

In the mid-1970s, a clutch of documentary-style pop films revealed a darker, cynical tone – a kind of adult riposte to the joy in the moment of *AHDN*. *That'll Be the Day*, starring real-life pop star David Essex, follows the career rise of Jim MacLaine, a John Lennon-like musician, from grammar school to holiday camps to pop stardom, but his selfish and abusive behaviour is filmed with an unflinching gaze by Michael Apted, who'd made his name with the *UP* documentary series that began in 1964 with *Seven Up!*. Ringo Starr was critically acclaimed for his gritty performance as the hero's friend, nine years after playing the loveable clown of *AHDN*. But he declined the sequel, *Stardust* (1974), apparently unhappy about aspects of the story, and was replaced by Adam Faith. According to critic Michael Brooke, this was because a key subplot was too close to the real-life story of drummer Pete Best's departure from the Beatles.[120]

Slade in Flame (1975), a fictional biopic of a hit band 'Flame', made close to the height of Slade's real chart success, combines beautiful cinematography with the PR cynicism of *Privilege*, and gangster violence closer to *Get Carter* (1971) than the joy of *AHDN*. 'Do you like what we do?' one of the band asks Tom Conti's PR manager on their first meeting. 'My personal preference really doesn't come into it,' he admits, candidly, comparing himself to a non-smoker who's a great success at selling cigarettes. In contrast to the *AHDN*-style romp Slade's manager (ex-Animals member) Chas Chandler wanted, the band went for a very dark film, much of it shot on location in Nottingham and Sheffield, and based on real incidents that had happened to them or to bands they knew. Its young director, Richard Loncraine, had come from factual TV, directing the popular BBC1 science series *Tomorrow's World* (1965–2003).

Set in the late 1960s, the film's arc heads fearlessly all the way to live concert footage and fan hysteria, followed closely by disillusioned disbanding. It is self-consciously the anti-*AHDN*, notably in a scene when the band, boorishly rather than charmingly, mess with their food and upset the toffs in the first-class carriage on their way down to London. As Noddy Holder recalled: 'It shows a naive band coming from the North, down on a train, in first class as you say, [and shows] that we weren't at ease. We were behaving like "yobbos".'[121] The film was a commercial disaster given their mostly teenage fans, but is now regarded as a cult masterpiece.

The knockabout speed of Lester's two Beatles films inspired most obviously *The Monkees* (1966–8) – a TV comedy show about a pop group, featuring lots of chases and slapstick to great songs. Although it's been claimed co-producer Bob Rafelson had the idea of a pop group TV show before *AHDN*,[122] it was the success of Lester's films that got the project off the ground. Micky Dolenz, Davy Jones, Mike Nesmith and Peter Tork, who responded to the advert in Hollywood trade journals in September 1965 for '4 insane boys age 17–21', were capable musicians and actors and became a successful group, though it took a long while for them to earn respect for their musicianship and songwriting, given the band's origins and studio control. The Monkees' self-aware and psychedelically charged feature film *Head* (1968), directed by Rafelson, was groundbreaking. John Patterson suggests *Head*, 'cynical and surreal, may be the best pop group movie after *AHDN*, but' – wrongly, I think – 'also the genre's death knell'.[123] Years later *AHDN*'s mix of pop vérité and actors continues to generate occasionally delightful surprises.

Lasse Hallström reused the formula of *AHDN* (documentary, concert footage, surreal fantasy sequences around a flimsy comedy plot about a radio journalist seeking an interview) for *ABBA: The Movie* (1977) to capture the hysteria around one of the then biggest bands in the world. A record of a phenomenon, but without the charisma or sexual charge of the Beatles. I remember being taken to see it in the cinema, hugely excited, two years before I ever saw *AHDN*, and I was deeply disappointed and bored.

AHDN's most self-conscious copy came in the Spice Girls' film *Spice World* (1997). The timing was significant: the band were riding the crest of a wave of newspaper-backed popularity, part of a self-aware 'Cool Britannia', an echo of the Swinging Sixties. We even had a new Labour prime minister (Tony Blair) elected in May that year, like Harold Wilson in October 1964, and the Spice Girls were the closest we'd had to the Beatles for years – gobby lasses, two from the north, with distinctive personalities and nicknames, who seemed a genuine girl gang, even if they had been put together by a pop Svengali.

Such was their fame and the media goodwill that, as a young BBC news correspondent, I was commissioned by the World Service to make a special TV news report about 'girl power' – a supposedly new, youthful feminism they were credited with inventing. *Spice World* is full of attempts at Lester-esque surrealism and cameos from the world of light entertainment, with Michael Barrymore channelling Victor Spinetti as a military dance teacher. But it was a poor offering, confirming only that *AHDN* was not a formula that could be easily replicated.

Perhaps *AHDN*'s greatest direct descendant – its Irish grandchild, even – is the sweary, sex and drug-filled *Kneecap* (2024), which won a BAFTA for outstanding British debut for its director and co-writer Rich Peppiatt. A fictionalised portrayal of the rise of the Northern Irish hip-hop trio, the eponymous film combines exhilarating real concert footage with rich humour and a surreal sense of the political discomfort caused by their proud Irish nationalist identity and Gaelic-language rapping.[124] The Beatles talking Scouse was controversial, but not like this! It's no coincidence, in my view, that Peppiatt's own background is in documentary news journalism. And what is Michael Fassbender, who plays the missing paramilitary father of one of the group, other than a refreshingly provocative take on Wilfrid Brambell's Grandfather?

At time of writing in 2025, the guitar band, of which the Beatles were the template, seems to have had its day. The most successful English-language artists in the world are solo performers, particularly women such as Taylor Swift. And their cinematic offerings have been highly polished concert films, more inspired by Madonna's *In Bed with Madonna* (1991), a documentary record of her Blond Ambition tour. Perhaps part of the nostalgic power of *AHDN* now is that it captures not just the Beatles in their prime, but an entire archetype that has passed.

While *AHDN* endures as a landmark of cinema, the future beckons. As new technologies emerge, the theatrical show ABBA Voyage suggests the possibility one day of an immersive virtual-reality Beatles experience, with far better sound quality than anyone experienced at an original concert, something *AHDN* did in its own way, with its presentation of the concert finale. The success of Peter Jackson's *Get Back* films, revisiting the *Let It Be* footage, has opened up new possibilities for rejuvenating the authentic documentary past for the present. It is an interesting coincidence that before *Get Back*, he used his newly developed technology for restoring archive material in the documentary film *They Shall Not Grow Old* (2018) to bring alive lost faces from World War I.

For a film driven entirely by *joie de vivre*, there is something inevitably melancholic about watching Richard Lester's *A Hard Day's Night* and the four young men at its heart. For, as long as the film exists, while we all grow old, we know they shall not grow old. And we will remember them.

Quatre garçons dans le vent (photograph by Bert Cann)

Notes

1 Bob Stanley, *Yeah Yeah Yeah: The Story of Modern Pop* (Faber & Faber, 2013), p. 123.
2 Alexander Walker, *Hollywood, England: The British Film Industry in the Sixties* (Michael Joseph, 1974), p. 462.
3 'The Beatles at Stowe School, Hugh Laurie on Agatha Christie', *Front Row*, BBC Radio 4, 3 April 2023.
4 Film producer Walter Shenson announces the new Beatles film in the *Daily Mail*, 31 October 1963.
5 Author interview, 'Anne-Marie Duff, Al Murray, Melvyn Hayes, Billboard Art', *Front Row*, BBC Radio 4, 15 July 2024.
6 *Men Only* was relaunched in 1971 by Paul Raymond and became a more explicit porn magazine.
7 Mark Lewisohn, *Radio Times Guide to TV Comedy* (BBC Worldwide, 1998), p. 638.
8 Author interview, 28 November 2024. Panel discussion at screening of *Beatles '64* at the Curzon Mayfair, London.
9 *A Hard Day's Night* 50th anniversary DVD extras (Second Sight, 2014).
10 Joel Morris, *Be Funny or Die: How Comedy Works and Why it Matters* (Unbound, 2024), p. 263.
11 *AHDN* 50th anniversary DVD extras.
12 In 1957 conscription was ended for those born after 1939. Both Ringo and John were born in 1940.
13 John makes a face he regularly pulled in real life that appears to mimic a person with disabilities, a common act at the time.
14 Boyd's blonde, knee-socked look was soon replicated by Julie Christie in *Darling* (1965) and by real-life sixth-former Marianne Faithfull, photographed by Gered Mankowitz (1964).
15 *AHDN* 50th anniversary DVD extras.
16 Steven Soderbergh, *Getting Away With It* (Faber & Faber, 1999), p. 30.
17 *AHDN* 50th anniversary DVD extras.
18 In real life, John's mother had been dead for five years, killed in a road crash. Earlier, on the train, Paul refers to his mother sending Grandfather along: 'My mother thought a trip would do him good.' Paul's real-life mother had died eight years earlier when Paul was fourteen.
19 Soderbergh, *Getting Away with It*, p. 30.
20 *AHDN* 50th anniversary DVD extras.
21 Neil Sinyard has compared the figure to the middle-aged police officer who appears at the end of Gene Kelly's frolics after his rain dance in *Singin' in the Rain* (1952). Neil Sinyard, *The Films of Richard Lester* (Barnes & Noble Books, 1985), p. 26.
22 Author interview (singer wanted to remain anonymous), 19 April 2025.
23 David E. Williams, 'Gilbert Taylor, BSC is Given the Spotlight with the ASC's International Achievement Award', *American Cinematographer*, February 2006. Available at: <https://theasc.com/magazine/feb06/taylor/page1.html> (accessed 5 July 2025).
24 Michael Bonner, 'The Making of *A Hard Day's Night*: "The Fans Had Got Hacksaws ..."', *Uncut*, 5 October 2015. Available at: <https://www.uncut.co.uk/features/the-making-of-a-hard-days-night-the-fans-had-got-hacksaws-71060/> (accessed 5 July 2025).
25 Walker, *Hollywood, England*, p. 238.
26 Author interview, 26 February 2025.

27 The Cast Iron Shore is mentioned in the lyrics to the Beatles song 'Glass Onion' (1968).
28 Paul Du Noyer, 'A *Hard Day's Night*: Behind the Camera', *MOJO* no. 108, November 2002. Available at: <https://www.pauldunoyer.com/a-hard-days-night-behind-the-camera/> (accessed 6 July 2025).
29 *AHDN* 50th anniversary DVD commentary.
30 Author interview, 22 January 2025.
31 Author interview, 3 April 2025.
32 *AHDN* 50th anniversary DVD extras.
33 Walker, *Hollywood, England*, p. 269.
34 *AHDN* 50th anniversary DVD extras.
35 Mark Lewisohn, *The Beatles A Hard Day's Night: A Private Archive* (Phaidon, 2016), p. 16.
36 *AHDN* 50th anniversary DVD extras.
37 '"I Don't Find Filmmaking Fun at All": A 1973 Interview with Richard Lester', *Sight and Sound* vol. 42, no. 2, Spring 1973. Available at: <https://www.bfi.org.uk/sight-and-sound/interviews/i-dont-find-filmmaking-fun-all-1973-interview-with-richard-lester> (accessed 6 July 2025).
38 Soderbergh, *Getting Away with It*, p. 10.
39 Interview transcript Lester with Philip Oakes (1967) during post-production of *How I Won the War*, p. 8, BFI National Archive.
40 'RHM Nimble: Lunch Date' advert, 1961. Available at: <https://player.bfi.org.uk/free/film/watch-rhm-nimble-lunch-date-1961-online> (accessed 6 July 2025).
41 Mark Lewisohn album sleeve notes to the Beatles, *The Beatles – Anthology 1* (Apple Records, 1995).

42 Lewisohn, *The Beatles A Hard Day's Night*, p. 19.
43 *AHDN* 50th anniversary DVD extras.
44 J. Philip di Franco (ed.), *The Beatles in Richard Lester's A Hard Day's Night: A Complete Pictorial Record of the Movie* (Penguin Books, 1978), p. xv.
45 Soderbergh, *Getting Away with It*, p. 106.
46 *AHDN* 50th anniversary DVD extras.
47 Di Franco (ed.), *The Beatles in Richard Lester's A Hard Day's Night*, p. xv.
48 Lewisohn, *The Beatles A Hard Day's Night*, p. 21.
49 Soderbergh, *Getting Away with It*, p. 15.
50 Lewisohn, *The Beatles A Hard Day's Night*, p. 21.
51 Ibid.
52 *AHDN* 50th anniversary DVD extras.
53 Soderbergh, *Getting Away with It*, p. 29.
54 Lewisohn, *The Beatles A Hard Day's Night*, p. 21.
55 Paul McCartney, *The Lyrics* (Penguin Books, 2021), p. 280.
56 Du Noyer, 'A *Hard Day's Night*: Behind the Camera'.
57 Barry Norman, 'Beatles to Star in Film About Beatles', *Daily Mail*, 31 October 1963.
58 The Beatles, *The Beatles Anthology* (Cassell & Co., 2000), p. 112.
59 Du Noyer, 'A *Hard Day's Night*: Behind the Camera'.
60 *AHDN* 50th anniversary DVD extras.
61 Ibid.
62 David Hurn, 'The Beatles Behind the Scenes – by the Photographer Who Saw it All', *Sunday Times*, 28 June 2024. Available at: <https://www.thetimes.com/magazines/the-sunday-times-magazine/article/

beatles-music-photographs-hard-days-night-7zw7wl885> (accessed 6 July 2025).

63 This and following quotes taken from *AHDN* 50th anniversary DVD extras.

64 I am indebted for location dates to Mark Lewisohn's *The Complete Beatles Chronicle* (Pyramid Books, 1992), and Piet Schreuders, Mark Lewisohn and Adam Smith's *The Beatles' London: A Guide to 467 Beatles Sites in and Around London* (Portico Books, 2008).

65 'The Beatles Interview: "We can't do the same thing all the time"', ITN interview, 16 October 1963. Available at: <https://www.youtube.com/watch?v=RuDdSxaISI8> (accessed 7 July 2025).

66 It's a fun coincidence, or possibly deliberate joke, that Lester incorporated a gag in his opening sequence using the same Marylebone station milk machine that Schlesinger featured in the closing sequence of *Billy Liar*. Norm is seen trying to open his carton, while Billy buys it as a delaying tactic.

67 *AHDN* 50th anniversary DVD extras.

68 The card is held on loan in the British Library.

69 Soderbergh, *Getting Away with It*, p. 34.

70 Lewisohn, *The Beatles A Hard Day's Night*, p. 20.

71 Du Noyer, 'A Hard Day's Night: Behind the Camera'.

72 Surprisingly, Lester has assured Mark Lewisohn that the train carriage sequence with the Richard Vernon gent was in fact revoiced post-sync. Mark Lewisohn interviews with Richard Lester 3 November 2014 and 18 June 2015.

73 The Beatles, *The Beatles Anthology*, p. 129.

74 Ian MacDonald, *Revolution in the Head: The Beatles' Records and the Sixties* (Pimlico, 1995), p. 90.

75 Lewisohn, *The Complete Beatles Chronicle*, p. 155.

76 This world of live TV mishaps was amiably captured in Norman Jewison's comedy *The Thrill of It All* (1963), scripted by Lester's contemporary, Carl Reiner, and starring Doris Day.

77 Hunter Davies, *The Beatles Book* (Ebury Press, 2016), p. 867.

78 'Now and Then: Richard Lester (1967)', interview with Bernard Braden, BFI Screenonline. Available at: <http://www.screenonline.org.uk/tv/id/1375204/index.html> (accessed 31 July 2025).

79 Davies, *The Beatles Book*, p. 818.

80 *AHDN* 50th anniversary DVD extras.

81 Cynthia Lennon, *John* (Hodder & Stoughton, 2006), p. 192.

82 Michael Sragow, 'Another "Hard Day's Night"', *Salon*, 7 December 2000. Available at: <https://www.salon.com/2000/12/07/hard_days_night_2/> (accessed 7 July 2025).

83 *AHDN* 50th anniversary DVD extras.

84 Bonner, 'The Making of A Hard Day's Night'.

85 *AHDN* 50th anniversary DVD extras.

86 The Beatles, *The Beatles Anthology*, p. 144.

87 Cecil Wilson, *Daily Mail*, 7 July 1964.

88 Dilys Powell, *Sunday Times*, 12 July 1964.

89 Isabel Quigley, *The Spectator*, July 1964.

90 Arthur Knight, *Saturday Review*,
19 September 1964.
91 Felix Barker, 'At Last – I Scream for
the Beatles', *London Evening News*,
9 July 1964.
92 Leonard Mosley, *Daily Express*,
7 July 1964.
93 Michael Thornton, *Sunday Express*,
12 July 1964.
94 *News of the World*, 12 July 1964.
95 Patrick Gibbs, *Daily Telegraph*,
7 July 1964.
96 *The Times*, 7 July 1964.
97 *Financial Times*, 10 July 1964.
98 *Monthly Film Bulletin*, August 1964.
99 Anne Scott James, *Daily Mail*,
16 July 1964.
100 Andrew Sarris, 'Bravo Beatles!',
Village Voice, 27 August 1964, p. 13.
101 'Yeah? Yeah. Yeah!', *Time* magazine,
4 August 1964.
102 *AHDN* 50th anniversary DVD extras.
103 Ibid.
104 'Hard Day's Night for a Girl
of Seven', *Sunday Express*, 23 August
1964.
105 Walker, *Hollywood, England*, p. 241.
106 Stephen Glynn, *A Hard Day's Night:
Turner Classic Movies British Film Guide*
(I. B. Tauris, 2004), p. 30.
107 *AHDN* is now seen as a fine early
example of *Blödel Syncro* – the German
art of dubbing original comedy
dialogue onto foreign films. Perhaps
partly thanks to all the arthouse film
references, *Der Spiegel* described it as
a 'pleasant surprise for cineastes',
'Yeah! Yeah! Yeah! (England)',
Der Spiegel, 25 August 1964.
108 Lewisohn, *The Beatles A Hard Day's
Night*, p. 64.
109 The Beatles, *The Beatles Anthology*,
pp. 167–8.
110 Ibid., p. 167.
111 *Superman II* (1980) and *Superman III*
(1983).
112 McCartney, *The Lyrics*, p. 52.
113 The Beatles, *The Beatles Anthology*,
p. 96.
114 George Harrison, *I, Me, Mine*
(Phoenix, 2004), p. 39.
115 'Ask a Filmmaker: Richard Lester'
(BFI, 2012). Available at: <https://
www.youtube.com/watch?v=6WMm-
eYXyLY&t=25s> (accessed 7 July 2025).
116 Keith Badman, *The Beatles Diary
Vol. 2: After the Break-up 1970–2001*
(Omnibus Press, 1999), p. 19.
117 *AHDN* 50th anniversary DVD extras.
118 In footage of the *NME* Poll
Winners' Concert at Wembley
Empire Pool in April 1965, when the
Beatles won several awards, you
can hear the audience of children
and teenagers booing loudly when
Savile comes on stage. Available
at: <https://www.youtube.com/
watch?v=BieoyTzP8aQ&t=1253s>
(accessed 7 July 2025).
119 Author interview, 'John Boorman,
Anya Gallaccio, The Halfway Kid
Performs', *Front Row*, BBC Radio 4,
23 September 2024.
120 Michael Brooke, 'Stardust (1974)',
BFI Screenonline. Available at: <http://
www.screenonline.org.uk/film/
id/495155/index.html> (accessed
7 July 2025).
121 Author interview, 'Noddy Holder
of Slade, Stephen Rea and Simone de
Beauvoir', *Front Row*, BBC Radio 4,
29 April 2025.

122 A. D. Amorosi, 'Micky Dolenz on How Bob Rafelson Used the Monkees to Help Create a Looser, Hip "New Hollywood"', *Variety*, 25 July 2022. Available at: <https://variety.com/2022/film/news/micky-dolenz-bob-rafelson-monkees-appreciation-head-1235324982/> (accessed 13 July 2025).

123 John Patterson, 'A *Hard Day's Night*: The Only Worthwhile Beatlemania Movie', *Guardian Guide*, 30 June 2014. Available at: <https://www.theguardian.com/music/2014/jun/30/a-hard-days-night-the-only-worthwhile-beatlemania-movie? (accessed 7 August 2025).

124 The band have remained politically controversial. Singer Liam Óg Ó hAnnaidh, charged under the name Liam O'Hanna, was accused of displaying a flag in support of proscribed organisation Hezbollah at a London gig, but the case was dismissed due to a technical error. As of October 2025 the Crown Prosecution Service had appealed this decision. A police investigation over comments the band made on stage at Glastonbury in June 2025 was dropped.

Credits

A Hard Day's Night
UK/USA
1964

Directed by
Richard Lester
Original Screenplay
Alun Owen
Produced by
Walter Shenson

© 1964 Proscenium
Films Ltd

Associate Producer
Denis O'Dell
Director of Photography
Gilbert Taylor
Musical Director
George Martin
Songs
John Lennon
Paul McCartney
Art Director
Ray Simm
Editor
John Jympson
Assistant Director
John D. Merriman
Camera Operator
Derek V. Browne
Costume Designer
Julie Harris
Beatles' Wardrobe
Dougie Millings & Son
Make-up
John O'Gorman
Hairdressing
Betty Glasow
Continuity
Rita Davison

Titles Design
Robert Freeman
Sound Recording
H. L. Bird
Stephen Dalby
Sound Editor
Gordon Daniel
Assistant Editor
Pamela Tomling

uncredited
United Artists
Production Executive
George 'Bud' Ornstein
Production Secretary
Beryl Harvey
2nd Assistant Directors
Barrie Melrose
Alex Carver-Hill
3rd Assistant Director
Bob Howard
Casting Director
Irene Lamb
2nd Camera Operator
Jack Atcheler
Camera Operator
Paul Wilson
Focus Puller
Roy Ford
Clapper/Loader
Peter Ewens
Stills Photography
Bert Cann
2nd Assistant Editor
Roy Benson
Assistant Art Director
George Lack
Draughtsman
William Alexander
Boom Operator
Don Wortham

Boom Assistant
Frank Sloggett
Sound Camera Operator
Mike Silverlock
Sound Editor
Jim Roddan
Publicity Director
Tony Howard
Executive Producer
David V. Picker

CAST
John Lennon
John
Paul McCartney
Paul
George Harrison
George
Ringo Starr
Ringo
Wilfrid Brambell
Grandfather
Norman Rossington
Norm
John Junkin
Shake
Victor Spinetti
TV director
Anna Quayle
Millie
Deryck Guyler
police inspector
Richard Vernon
man on train
Eddie Malin
hotel waiter
Robin Ray
TV floor manager
Lionel Blair
TV choreographer

Alison Seebohm
secretary
David Janson
(as David Jaxon)
young boy

uncredited
Pattie Boyd
Jean, schoolgirl on train
Prue Berry
schoolgirl on train
Terry Hooper
casino croupier
Jeremy Lloyd
club dancer
Michael Trubshawe
club manager
Marianne Stone
society reporter
Derek Nimmo
Leslie Jackson
Dougie Millings
tailor
Kenneth Haigh
Simon Marshall, shirt
advertising man
Julian Holloway
Adrian
Susan Whitman
Susan
David Langton
actor
Claire Kelly
barmaid

John Bluthal
car thief
Tina Williams
Tina
Terry Brooks
urchin
Phil Collins
boy in audience
Bridget Armstrong
head of make-up
Brian Epstein
man in crowd
Rosemarie Frankland
showgirl
Susan Brown
Ric Hutton
Hedger Wallace
Heather Bishop
Anne Clune
journalist
Paula Smyczok
Lavinia Lang
Martin Gadd
Philip Gadd
Andrea Brett
Peter Newton
Patricia Newton
Dani Sheridan
Edina Ronay
girl at disco
Roger Avon
policeman
Margaret Nolan
woman at casino
Jane Lumb

Production Details
35mm
1.66:1
Black and white
Mono
Running time:
87 minutes

Release Details
UK theatrical release
on 7 July 1964 by
United Artists
US theatrical release
on 12 August 1964 by
United Artists

Select Bibliography

Beatles, The, *The Beatles Anthology* (Cassell & Co., 2000).

Davies, Hunter, *The Beatles Book* (Ebury Press, 2016).

Di Franco, J. Philip (ed.), *The Beatles in Richard Lester's A Hard Day's Night – A Complete Pictorial Record of the Movie* (Chelsea House Publisher, 1977).

Lennon, Cynthia, *John* (Hodder & Stoughton, 2005).

Lewisohn, Mark, *The Complete Beatles Chronicle* (Pyramid Books, 1992).

Lewisohn, Mark, *The Beatles A Hard Day's Night: A Private Archive* (Phaidon, 2016).

Schreuders, Piet, Mark Lewisohn and Adam Smith, *The Beatles' London: A Guide to 467 Beatles Sites in and Around London* (Portico Books, 2008).

Walker, Alexander, *Hollywood, England: The British Film Industry in the Sixties* (Michael Joseph, 1974).